Sons of Israel, Sons of God

Robert Carroll
and
Tom Sangster-Wilson

Marshall Pickering

Marshall Morgan and Scott
Marshall Pickering
3 Beggarwood Lane, Basingstoke, Hants RG23 7LP, UK

Copyright © 1987 By Robert Carroll
First published in 1987 by Marshall Morgan and Scott Publications Ltd
Part of the Marshall Pickering Holdings Group
A subsidiary of the Zondervan Corporation

British Library CIP Data

Carroll, Robert
    Sons of Israel, sons of God.
    1. Witness bearing (Christianity)
    I. Title.   II. Swift, Catherine
    248'.5'   BV4520
        ISBN 0-551-01436-9

Text Set in Plantin by Brian Robinson, Buckingham.
Printed in Great Britain by Hazell Watson & Viney Ltd,
Member of the BPCC Group, Aylesbury, Bucks.

Contents

Preface

One of the most powerful and eloquent speakers in church history was *undoubtedly* the Apostle Paul. He would indeed have captivated our world of today! And yet, his most effective impact was ever and always his testimony as to how he – a 'Hebrew of Hebrews' – met the 'King of the Jews'. Of such a character is this excellent book, it illustrates most vividly how, after almost 2,000 years, both Jew and Gentile are meeting the Messiah in ever-increasing numbers.

No experience is more vital than the life-changing moment when we are reconciled to the God of creation and redemption through faith in Jesus our Lord. The reality and the blindness of this experience comes through most impressively and refreshingly in this book.

You will find, as I did, warmth and encouragement in the wonder of God's power unfolding in the lives of both Jew and Gentile.

Ald Ridpath
Chairman Prayer for Israel.

Foreword

This book is a remarkable fulfilment of that precious portion of the Word of God, Ephesians 2:11-18, illustrating with perfect detail how Gentiles – aliens from the Commonwealth of Israel and strangers to the covenants of promise without hope or God in this world, far off from salvation and Christ, have been brought near to God, and to the Jew, by the blood of Christ. He who is our peace has broken down that wall of prejudice, suspicion, indifference, hostility and antisemitism – a wall of division and separation between Jew and Gentile, making us new men in attitude, purpose and fellowship (v. 14). Christ made reconciliation and peace possible, by his cross, thus making us one body, his Church. Christ's death on the cross brings about the death of enmity between Gentile and Jew, not by example, but by atonement for sin, as God's lamb sacrifice and the shedding of his blood, without which there is no remission of sins (vv 15-16).

Christ's sacrifice preached peace to those far off – the Gentiles – and those near – the Jews – who knew the revelation of God's purposes through their history. It is through Christ – Yeshua Ha' Meshiach – that Jewish and Gentile believers have access to the Father, by one Spirit, in one Body, his redeemed Church (vv. 17-18).

It is my rich joy, pleasure and experience to work with both Robert Carroll, the Gentile, and Tom Sangster-Wilson, the Jew. Together we seek to edify the Church to know God's purposes for Israel, to pray for the peace of Jerusalem and the salvation of Israel. We seek the Lord together, in one Spirit serving him as he shapes his plans to fulfil his word in these end times.

This book will help Gentile Christians to understand the background of Jewish life and culture and their suffering at the hands of the so-called Church. It will show Gentile Christians their indebtedness to the Jewish race as the vehicle for the revelation of God, and the Messiah-Redeemer – Christ.

I heartily commend this book to Jewish people who will realise there are Christians who love them and pray for Israel. I commend it to Gentile Christians that they may seek to repay their debt to the Jew (Rom. 15:27). Here is a story of a Gentile believer and a Jewish believer, serving together the God of Israel.

Don Hender

PART I
TO THE JEW

1: Hebrew Inheritance

It was a warm, sunny morning. One of those summer days when all seems well with the world – and especially with your own. Yet it took just one second for my contentment to be shattered as the stout, wooden door opened and a burly police-officer walked into the building.

For a moment he stood eyeing the room and its occupants, casting only a cursory glance in my direction but it was enough to chill my blood. When he began to talk to the people closest to him I froze. From his attitude and the way they responded, it was quite obvious he was asking questions. But what questions? Some of these people knew nothing of my past.

At the memory of all my misdeeds I went hot and clammy. The throbbing pulse in my ears was deafening as my heart beat faster and threatened to break loose from my quaking body. There must be something I've overlooked, I thought. Instantly a horrifying vision presented itself; one of being arrested in public to be bundled into a waiting police-van and then whisked away to some bare, lonely cell.

It could only have been morbid curiosity which urged me to go over to him. He was in full uniform and when the glitter from his helmet badge caught my attention, I fixed my gaze on to it while trying to gather my senses.

It seemed to take years for my feet to cover the few yards dividing me from my tormentor. Years during which, like the proverbial drowning man, my entire past life flashed before my eyes.

I was born at the family pawnshop on a street corner in the heart of Liverpool's Jewish community. The date was November 1st, 1935, a time when war clouds were gathering over Europe and the streets of Germany's third Reich echoed to the sound of military bands, Nazi jackboots and screams for Jewish blood.

My name is Tom Sangster-Wilson, part Jewish, part Scottish from my father's side. However, the Jewish family line is always passed down through the distaff side.

This tradition was introduced in the days of the crusaders when many Jewish girls produced children sired by them either as a result of fraternising or rape. Having just one Jewish parent qualifies a child to be a Jew. And as it is a natural fact that there can never be absolute certainty of the father's identity, so too can there never be any doubt as to who gives birth. Thus the mother's line is the one to follow in the Hebrew faith and my mother, Aida, had some illustrious orthodox connections. Her line could be traced back to the Levites; one of the original tribes set aside by God for priestly duties, a fact which was naturally the source of much family pride. By tradition also, a mother takes on the role of teaching her children the culture, conventions and basic fundamentals of Judaism.

My maternal grandfather, Isaach Harris Rosenberg, had been born in Palestine but while he was still an infant his parents went to live in Russia.

When he reached manhood he married Aida Cohen but due to the persecution of Jews in Russia he returned with his young bride to Palestine. There my mother Aida was born in Tel Aviv and while she was still a child, they moved again. This time it was to England where they took a tailoring business in Liverpool.

With her consent, when she was only sixteen years old, they arranged my mother's first marriage to Hans Glasman, a young Liverpool pawnbroker who lived two doors from the tailor's shop. Hans also owned a guest house he'd inherited from his parents. This was situated two doors away in the other direction from the pawn-shop.

When Hans died in early middle-age, Aida was left with seven children – whose ages ranged from five to fifteen – and with two businesses to run. Obviously she was far from destitute, but she realised that, with her sizeable brood to rear, the money could soon be dissipated. Somehow, she must combine being a mother of seven with being a successful businesswoman. Consequently her life was absorbed with caring for her young family, attending to the pawn-shop and supervising the running of the guest house. And it was here where she met and fell desperately in love with my father, Tom Sangster-Wilson.

Tom was a boxer from the Gorbals district of Glasgow in Scotland. He was of Jewish stock but his family had been converted to Christianity. His father had become a Methodist minister and made it his life's mission to collect money to help bring Jews from out of Russia.

Tom was a highly intelligent man whose parents had hoped to send him to university. But he rebelled against this so strongly he left home. That was in 1930 – the onset of the *depression*, and a time of great poverty and deprivation. Unemployment was rife, people were starving and Tom was forced to travel around the country literally *fighting* for his living. At the time of taking up lodgings in my mother's guest house he was fulfilling an engagement at the Liverpool Stadium close by.

He was a good looking, five foot eleven inches blond Adonis of twenty-two, some nine years younger than my mother, a tall, attractive woman of ample figure with deep-tanned skin and large, brown eyes.

After a while, Aida's parents began to suspect her relationship with this lodger, Tom, was more than platonic. Yet, as they couldn't be *sure*, they refrained from commenting on it. Sometime later when she told them she was going to marry him they exploded with anger. They had originally arranged a good marriage for her with Hans Glasman and suggested that, if she really needed a husband's support and companionship, *they* would find someone suitable for her.

Aida pointed out that she was no longer sixteen. She was a widow, mother of seven children and a businesswoman who could manage her own future. Although they'd always acknowledged her strong will, they were furious when she rejected their offer of help and demanded an explanation. Then Aida shocked them into deeper anger when she told them not only was she in love with Tom – she was pregnant.

My grandparents had all the typical Jewish colouring and physical attributes, grandmother being of medium height and figure, grandfather rather a small man. Grandmother could often be vicious in tongue and actions. She was also over protective and very possessive towards her family. Grandfather was a shrewd old man with just the suggestion of a hard streak in his otherwise benevolent nature. His pious living and high standards always maintained a serenity in the family. Now, he felt betrayed and immediately cast my mother's authority aside. From then on he considered her eldest son, Henry, by then aged seventeen, to be the head of *her* household.

But sadly, it wasn't only her parents who objected to this unlikely match. As soon as their mother's intentions were made known, Henry and his younger brother, David, aged sixteen, left home and moved in with their grandparents.

Still, the marriage went ahead without their blessings.

Following the wedding, the two older girls, Ruth and Naomi, also left home. I was born shortly after and the Sangster-Wilsons, together with the three remaining Glasman children, settled down to anything but a peaceful life.

Both my parents were of fiery disposition. Rows occurred

10

often with him bawling in his strong Scots accent while mother retaliated in Hebrew.

My grandparents weren't exactly *displeased* with this state of affairs. They'd predicted all sorts of disasters to the union as a punishment for Aida 'marrying out'. What they didn't realise, or didn't want to, was that my parents were happily married and very much in love despite the quarrels.

All the same, my father didn't always confine his temper to the home. He had given up his itinerant boxing life and managed to get work as general foreman on a local building site. Inevitably there was a time when he had—to put it delicately—an altercation with a work colleague which rapidly got out of hand. Forgetting his own strength and boxing skills he let fly, badly injuring the other man. Father was so filled with remorse, he volunteered to donate half his wages each week to support the man's wife and three children while their bread-winner was in hospital.

Oddly enough, the arguments that raged about the house were mostly centred around me, *their own child*.

The trouble began when I was only eight days old and was taken by my mother's family to the Synagogue for circumcision, a most solemn ceremony which can be performed only by a Mohel; the ritual circumciser.

This proved my mother hadn't renounced her Judaism when she married Tom and had assumed a Jewish wife's role; bringing up the children in strict Torah obedience—that is, following the teachings of the five Books of Moses.

Father was furious. He had no intention of allowing me to be brought up in the Hebrew faith, although he readily agreed his step-children should be.

Added to this controversy was the pressure put on them both by my grandparents. They hadn't cast my mother out of their lives for marrying a 'goy'—a derogatory term for Gentiles—although everyone, herself included, had assumed they would. Maybe it was because they didn't want to relinquish access to their grandchildren; and I was one of them even though they disapproved of my father.

Grandparents play a very influential part in Jewish life, their views and wishes always being respected. This created a great dilemma for my mother because they insisted I be brought up in strict Torah obedience. Father was equally adamant that I be brought up as a Gentile. And although my mother wanted me brought up in the Jewish faith she didn't want to give her parents the satisfaction of thinking they had succeeded where her husband hadn't.

I was as a rag between fighting dogs.

A few years later while my half-brother and sisters were going off each day to the King David school in the city, I was kept at home to be instructed well away from all Hebrew influence.

The truant officer, or 'school board' as he was commonly known, began making frequent visits to the house only to be informed that I was being educated at home.

Although I was only five at the time, this state of affairs tended to separate me from the other children not only physically but emotionally. They resented my staying at home. I resented being treated differently from them. We didn't even look like siblings; me with my blond hair, light skin and blue eyes they with their swarthy colouring.

Time and observation have made me realise the rivalry between my father and his father-in-law wasn't a personal thing at all. Under other circumstances the two men would probably have liked each other. After all they weren't that different in their characteristics. No, apart from the religious gap, their intolerance of each other came from the influence each wanted to have on my mother. It was such a wasted enmity. If only they could have seen through their hostility, they would have understood that Aida Sangster-Wilson had a mind of her own. And it was a more determined one than their two put together. Grandfather was busy playing the role of archetypal patriarch in the family. Father was acting out his part of Scottish master in his own home.

And all the time, mother was staunchly holding on to her Hebrew right to bring up *all* her offspring in the manner she believed right. Like any other mother telling her children of their inheritance, she taught me about the Holy scriptures, the prophets and the land of Israel.

It was one of those silly situations where an outsider could so easily step in and point out the simple facts to each protagonist – but no one ever does.

It took the coming of war in 1939 to restore an element of peace to our home. In 1940 my father was called into the army and it seemed he'd no sooner stepped on to the train at Lime Street station, than my grandfather had me enrolled at the King David School along with the other children. Naturally, this drew the entire family close again. Once more mother was recognised as having sole rule over her household and my future was resolved – for the time being at least.

The great sadness in all this was, my father wasn't sharing in the new found tranquillity. But then again, had he been there, there wouldn't have been any.

However, Grandpa Isaach's cunning and triumph didn't last long. Trouble flared again when my father came home for his first leave and discovered that I was a pupil at the King David School. Immediately, he had me transferred to the Gentile, West Derby Village School.

My grandfather, not to be outdone, went to see the headmaster and explained the situation. Although he couldn't deny my father the right to send me to that school, he could appeal against my being given Christian religious instruction and his wishes were respected. For the duration of my father's leave my Jewish, religious education was taken over by my grandparents in the privacy of their home.

When my father returned to his unit back I went to the King David School. The next leave I was sent back to the

13

West Derby Village School. Then back to the King David when he went away again.

Even at such an early age, I knew I was responsible for the lack of harmony between my parents. I would dearly have loved to tear myself in two simply to let each have their own way and stop the constant bickering when we were all together.

2: Birth of a Jew

In a time when most house and shop exteriors were painted mud brown or sludge green I suppose our pawnshop had a distinguished appearance with its red painted door and window-frames. Otherwise it was quite typical of its kind. One window held an array of unredeemed pledges while the glass in the other window was painted brown for half its height. This lent a certain amount of privacy to any transaction being made within the confines of the dimly lit interior.

Inside the shop was a glass fronted counter displaying many forfeited treasures; a collection of unrealised hopes and heartbreak.

Frequented by both Jew and non-Jew, pawnshops flourished during the 1930's recession.

Although viewed by many as a parasitic trade others saw it as an essential service to the community. For the temporary forfeiture of a best suit or some trinkets in exchange for a few coppers or shillings many a family, who would otherwise have gone hungry, were able to partake of a hearty meal.

Behind the shop, living quarters were reached through a long narrow hallway with rooms opening off to left and right. Downstairs accommodation comprised of a parlour, living room and kitchen or, as the latter were called in the north of England at that time, the kitchen and back-kitchen. It was a three storey building, the two upper floors being bedrooms and the bathroom, a rather austere place in those days, priorities being functional rather than luxury.

The house furnishing too was more for utility and family comfort than show because we were quite a large household.

Besides my parents and the children, there was an accumulation of pets. We had a black and white, smooth haired mongrel called Pongo; a very excitable animal who performed the 'wall of death' round the room whenever visitors arrived. This commotion would always invite a stream of Yiddish abuse from my mother and, for several minutes, chaos reigned.

We also had two black Persian cats; a grey parrot who spoke both fluent English and Hebrew and an unredeemed pledge in the form of a defiant, long-tailed green monkey called Malpa. He chattered constantly and, despite all efforts to coax him to live amongst us, insisted upon permanent residence atop the banister rail on the first landing. This position enabled him to fulfil his one desire in life, to attack and bite me at every opportunity. Had he lived anywhere else in the house I could, with some effort, have avoided him completely. Squatting on the banister as he did, I was forced to run the gauntlet whenever I went upstairs to either the bathroom or my bedroom. No one was sure why he hated me so much. Perhaps he sensed all the trouble in the house was the direct result of my existence. Maybe he objected to my fairness, although he showed no similar dislike of my father who had identical colouring.

There was one other inhabitant of our home, a brown bantam hen; sole property of my father. Like the monkey, it claimed its own special place of residence – perched on the back of his armchair by the fireside with a sheet of paper placed on the carpet immediately to its rear. There it stood on one leg, with one eye closed, glaring at my grandfather with the other whenever he visited us. For some unknown reason, its presence really disturbed him and it was an accepted fact that father only kept it to annoy him. This wasn't so much an extension of the animosity between the two men as an outlet for my father's impish sense of humour.

Throughout those war years, while he was away in the forces, Liverpool was frequently bombed by night and sometimes by day. Great portions of the city were destroyed and no one knew from one day to the next if they would survive the next bombardment.

Unless they were injured or lost their homes and loved ones, the blitz wasn't as terrifying an ordeal for children as it was for their parents. Adults have a greater sense of danger. For children war is often some kind of adventure and we were no exception. When the raids were on it didn't occur to us that we were in peril. Others perhaps, but not us.

Night after night, just as we were in our first sleep, the horrendous wail of the air-raid sirens would spring into life all over the city. With the inevitable grumbling we would be hauled back to consciousness and, still in pyjamas or nightdresses, we would hastily clamber into our cosy, fleecy-lined siren-suits; the forerunner of today's track-suit and designed by Winston Churchill himself.

Underneath the house was an enormous cellar rigged out as an air-raid shelter. My mother would quickly herd us all down there, together with the black and white dog, two black cats, the grey parrot, the little brown hen and Malpa, the green monkey – these were the only times he condescended to vacate his perch.

Besides the children and the animals there were my sisters, Ruth and Naomi, with my grandparents and several neighbours.

It was a warm, comfortable cellar although, on reflection, its protection was rather inadequate. At the time it seemed the ultimate in security and we felt much better off than those who used the municipal shelters in the streets or even people who had corrugated-metal Anderson shelters in their back-yards or gardens.

There were bunk-beds for the children, chairs for the grown-ups. We had lighting, heating, and facilities for making hot drinks. We had a radio and even a piano. Once we were all safely down there, in order to cover up the sounds of screaming bombs and crashing masonry, mother would play the piano and we would all be encouraged to sing. Some people wore ear-plugs which really were to drown out the sounds of war and bore no reflection upon either my mother's musical efforts nor those of the singers.

Everyone would have brought their gas-masks with them and I well remember my own Mickey Mouse mask. It had huge, black ears, a long black snout and yellow body. These were supplied to very young children as, being less sinister in appearance than the contraptions issued to adults, they helped to take some of the trauma out of those dreadful times we were living through.

It wasn't known to us then but even while we were enduring the horrors of the blitz, many of our relatives were experiencing much worse in Hitler's notorious concentration camps. Quite a number of them failed to survive the war.

By this time Henry and David had been called up to serve in the forces. At such a tender age, I wasn't able to appreciate the anxiety this must have caused my mother added to which would be her concern for my father.

Naturally, my grandparents would share her worries— even over my father no doubt. They weren't heartless. And although Ruth and Naomi had left home they were always grateful for the use of our air-raid shelter. I knew they'd left home because they didn't approve of my father but I didn't understand why. This was because I couldn't fully comprehend what it meant to be a Jew.

It was about this time that I had my first real taste of anti-semitism. We awoke one morning to discover huge letters in brown paint daubed all over the shop windows saying 'Jews go home' and 'Go home you * * * dirty Jews!'

Nearly all our friends and relative received the same treatment. Some had a flood of mail demanding that they leave the country at once or else . . .

This was all very mystifying to me. What did it all mean? Where did they expect us to go? We *were* at home.

Sometimes, whenever we strayed from the Jewish sector of the city, we would be called after in the street 'You * * * Christ killer' or 'You murdered Jesus'.

I even got this from some of the pupils at the Gentile school but it didn't make any sense to me. I knew Jesus was a Jewish Rabbi who had made claims to be God. Something which Jews couldn't accept. And because of this they had suffered so much from Christians that he was quite disliked by them – but we hadn't murdered him. How could we when he'd died many hundreds of years ago. And anyway the Gentile children were taught that the *Romans* had nailed him to a cross and killed him?

I was already attending the Synagogue by that time. And at home it was a natural part of life to observe all the festivals. September saw us celebrating Rosh Hashanah – the New Year. There was Yom Kippur when we fasted; Succoth; Chanukah; Purim; Passover and Shavuot.

We observed strict Kosher dietary laws. In our kitchen there was a set of cooking utensils, dishes and glasses which were never to be used except for the feast of Passover. This is when no food containing yeast or other raising agent is permitted to be in the house let alone eaten and no utensil or dish which has ever been in contact with it may be used.

Where a family was too poor to own a complete set of cooking and tableware for the purpose they would boil everything to ensure it was purified from all contamination with the prohibited food.

Only fish with fins and scales were fit for our consumption. All other seafood was forbidden.

Meat producing animals such as goats, deer, sheep and cattle which had cloven hoofs *and* chewed their food could be eaten. If an animal had only one of these characteristics, then it could not.

Although we were permitted to eat this meat there were still certain rituals to follow before it was totally approved. It had first to be soaked in water for a minimum of thirty minutes then left to drain. My mother would then sprinkle it liberally with salt and leave it for an hour. A final rinse would wash away the salt and any remaining blood and at last it was ready to cook. If at any time during this processing the meat happened to fall back into the rinsing water it could not be re-processed but must be thrown out immediately.

Another law was that meat and dairy produce must never be eaten together. If one was eating a meat sandwich, the bread could not be buttered. If meat was being eaten, milk could not be added to tea or coffee.

But of all things it was pork which carried the greatest taboo. I didn't know why. It was simply another rule in my life which I accepted without question.

Nevertheless, I couldn't understand all the fuss one day when I played a prank on my cousins. I was only seven at the time but I really believed that if my grandfather could catch me, he would kill me.

It was the school holidays, some of my cousins were visiting for the day and as it was a hot, sunny July we were all playing out in the street.

Our home bordered on Chinatown and one of my friends was Vinty Lowe from the nearby Chinese Laundry.

It was sheer boyish mischief that prompted him to go into his house and come out with a long piece of streaky bacon tied to a length of bamboo stick. When he handed it to me, without a moment's hesitation as to its significance, shouting and yelling to make as much din as possible, I began to chase everybody in sight – including my Jewish cousins.

They fled, screaming, and all the commotion brought

both my mother and grandpa Isaach to their shop doors. When my mother saw what I was doing, she bore down on me to give me such a slap on my legs that the stick, with its piece of bacon, shot out of my hand and flew across the road to land with a smack on grandpa Isaach's shoulder.

I can see him now, always in a dark suit with highly polished boots, he wore a short beard and I can never remember seeing him without his measuring tape around his neck.

On contact with the forbidden meat, he was so horrified he leapt up in the air — air which turned blue as he ranted and raved in a torrent of Russian and Yiddish threats.

One look at his face which had turned purple and I was off as fast as my legs would move. After a few hundred yards, I slackened my pace and turned to go back only to see he was still in pursuit. Despite his sixty-odd years, he was racing along like a young athlete. I turned again and ran, all the way to the Gladstone Docks, some three and a half miles away. There I managed to lose him in the hubbub of activity and sank down in a corner to regain my breath.

For the rest of the day, I wandered about, terrified to return home. It was late afternoon when this happened and, within the next half hour after the shop closed at five thirty, I would have been called in for tea. Now I was starving, thirsty and very frightened.

I had no idea of the time but as evening drew in, once the wartime blackout made itself evident and the dockside bustle subsided my nerves told me I couldn't stay there any longer. The comparative silence was eerie. Lengthening shadows conjured up all sorts of images and it seemed better to go home to be slaughtered by loved ones than to stay there and face goodness knew what.

Slowly I made my way along the dark, unfamiliar streets with only terror and a gnawing hunger to guide me in the direction of home. It was as I turned a street corner in the Islington district that my sister Ruth found me.

With a cry of relief she ran forward reaching out for my hand. For an instant I was tempted to struggle against her grasp and run away again but she was telling me how anxious everyone was. For hours they'd searched the area and were on the point of calling the police. I didn't believe her. She was taking me home to be beaten but by then I was too weary to care.

When we walked in to the house I was amazed to be greeted with tears, kisses and hugs. Only after a very welcome supper and when I was safely tucked up in bed did it suddenly occur to me; they really cared about me and grandpa Isaach hadn't killed me after all. I never wanted to see bacon again in my life though – and I still didn't know why all the fuss.

That was a lesson I would certainly never forget. The memory of it still causes me to cringe. And as for pork, for years the very sight of a pig filled me with the same horror my grandfather displayed when he was so reviled at its touch.

Not long after that episode, behind his shop in the storeroom where he kept all the bolts of cloth, grandpa taught me another hard lesson in life.

From my weekly pocket-money I'd managed to save up one shilling and sixpence (7½p), quite a large sum of money for a seven year old in 1942. I boasted so much about this nest-egg that grandpa coaxed me into playing a game of cards with him 'to see if I could double it'.

Within minutes he'd won all my money. I really expected he would give it back to me. But he didn't. He said that would teach me not to boast, not to gamble and never to trust anybody!

Like my father, grandpa Isaach also had a wry sense of humour and through it attempted to teach me another lesson. Always encouraged to be thrifty with the adage 'Take care of the pennies and the pounds will take care of themselves', I raced into his shop one day to tell him how

I'd saved a penny. 'Instead of *getting on* the bus, I ran all the way home behind it and saved my fare,' I proudly announced.

Grandad's response was to cuff me gently round the ear saying 'You should have run behind a taxi, then you would have saved half a crown'!

It was some months later when Judaism began to hold any real meaning for me. I had been to a morning service at the Church Road Synagogue in the Allerton district of Liverpool.

There were no bells ringing. They never do on the Jewish Shabbat – or Sabbath as the Gentiles call it – the day set aside from all secular activities in order to sanctify it as a special time of worship. It had been a good service with some of the young ones reciting short portions of scripture; a ritual part of Jewish life since the time of the prophets.

With the prayer at an end I was experiencing that satisfaction which always came from having obeyed the commands of the Hebrew scripture which repeatedly tells the people of Israel 'You must be holy'.

As I stood at the top of the cold, granite steps leading to the pavement I noticed my mother and the other parents were already some way along the street. I smiled to myself and reflected on her often used words. 'Tom,' she'd say, 'Holiness requires an act of separation. You must move from the ordinary to achieve the extraordinary.'

The morning was cold and blustery and a sudden gust of biting wind around my exposed knees jolted me from my thoughts. I glanced up at the sky; a wartime sky overcast as much by the blimp shapes of barrage-balloons as by cloud.

The rabbinic laws have always dictated that we should walk to and from the Synagogue and for this group of Torah-obedient Jews there was no exception. Still, there was always a degree of complaining from the older boys at having to walk the one mile home in 'these days of modern transport'.

It wasn't so much a protest against the distance as the unattractive route which took us past the drab outline and obnoxious fumes of the gas-works to say nothing of the many bombed areas. Those depressing sites belying the effectiveness of the silver-grey balloons, bobbing and floating on their cables way above our heads, to bring down enemy planes.

I fixed my gold-braid kippor firmly on the back of my head and walked down the steps to join my older half-brother, Charlie and some friends to set off on the cold trek home.

It was as we were nearing home that we caught the first glimpse of trouble. It came in the form of about twelve toughs who were blocking the pavement and spilling over into the road. They were much bigger and older than most of us and outnumbered us by about three to one. The grim expressions on their faces and their menacing stance announced that they were intent on creating havoc.

The tightening knot in the pit of my stomach told me there was no way of avoiding it.

I remembered the story of the Philistines greatly outnumbering the Israelites and of young David sorting them out with his sling. He'd achieved a victory then and, with this in mind, I went forward.

It was foolish because I was the youngest and the smallest of my group but the louts seemed to have singled me out. This is hardly surprising. It must have puzzled them to see me with my fair skin, blond hair and light blue eyes in the company of those young Jews. Yet, at the same time, in my Shabbat suit and with the kippor on my head, I was so clearly *one of them*.

For an instant we all glared and snarled at each other then, with fists, feet and heads hastily adapted as combat weapons, the battle was on.

At first my brother and friends attempted to form a shield around me until they realised I was fighting my way out of it to take my place in the *front line*. We seemed to be giving a good account of ourselves too until I saw a couple of my friends rolling along the cobbled street. This halted my actions for a moment then, with renewed anger, I braced myself for a fresh onslaught and selected my next target.

But suddenly, the fighting was over. Everyone seemed to petrify and gape wide-eyed at something behind me. Slowly I turned round to see what had brought such an abrupt end to the fracas.

A short distance away stood a woman. To a child of my years it was impossible to put an age on her but she was small in stature and slight of build. In her dark-brown mac and feathered hat with her brown shopping-bag, she presented a dowdy picture, yet, although she hadn't spoken a word her presence was enough to send shivers along the spine.

The warring rivals stood spellbound, looking at this unspectacular creature who had brought such violence to a dramatic end. Her sharp eyes quickly took in the scene and while everyone was still in a trance, her soft voice carried across the road.

'What do you think you are doing? Don't you know these are God's chosen children?'

Those few carefully selected words had more impact on the situation than a troop of cavalry charging at full speed down the road could have had.

I watched as, without a murmur or challenge of her authority, our assailants quietly sauntered away gathering speed to make a hasty retreat once they had placed fifty yards between themselves and our champion.

I felt compelled to scrutinise more closely the face of the woman who had come to our rescue but when I looked, there was no one in sight.

Until then I'd never thought of us Jews as being *special* or *chosen* people – simply different. Encounters like we'd just experienced were commonplace but then, the lame, the mentally retarded, spectacle wearers or even red-heads with freckles would qualify for verbal or physical abuse from such gangs. They were soon forgotten, yet somehow, I sensed this one would stay with me for a long time – due to a dowdy, little woman in a brown mac.

On hearing the battle from the next street, parents and friends had turned back to come running to our aid. By the time they reached us it was all over with both the enemy and our ally vanished from the scene.

We were left to dust down our Shabbat suits while trying to explain on the way home how we'd come by the grazes, bruises, scuffed shoes and torn clothes suffered in the scuffle.

3: In the Wilderness

Two years later the war ended and the whole world was rejoicing yet, ironically, it was a time of mixed blessings for me.

Over the past few years, my father had been posted abroad, serving in Egypt and Italy. With the war at an end he would soon be returning home and, although there was nothing I wanted more, this would mean the end of peace for me. There was only my youngest sister, Aida, still living with us and my father's homecoming would probably mean she would leave. All the old quarrels would start up again and I would be the butt of them.

Apart from the rows, there was something else to worry about. I was almost eleven years old and although my Barmitzvah was over two years away I already knew my destiny lay within the Hebrew faith. How could this be explained to my father while still expecting him to believe I loved him? He would never understand.

There was no opportunity to tell him. Maybe I didn't make one. I would have done anything to avoid unpleasantness between my parents and when he returned home and insisted I leave the King David School any protests from me would only have inflamed the situation.

Once more, I was to attend a Gentile school which was going to have a very unsettling effect upon me and I resented it bitterly. Thankfully, my mother was more stubborn than before and refused to send me there.

My father soon found employment as a builder's agent and each morning went off to work leaving my mother to deal with the truant officer who was again making regular visits to the house. This time he wasn't satisfied with the explanation that I was being educated at home. Because of this, it seemed there was a lot of trouble ahead for the Sangster-Wilson family. But then, quite suddenly, my father relented. I could stay on at the King David school. No matter what my mother wanted for me, it was all right with him.

It was many years before I learned the reason for this change of heart. On his demobilisation from the army, he learned that my mother was suffering from sugar diabetes, the 'Jewish Plague' as it's called. From then on, to save her from any further distress, he gave in on most issues, my education being one of them.

The biggest surprise was when my sister, Aida, then seventeen, arrived home one evening with a Gentile boyfriend and my mother ordered the pair of them from the house. I braced myself for one of the terrible old-time rows because my father considered himself to be a Gentile. But he uttered not one word of reproach.

The next potential upheaval in our family was when some Russian relatives came to visit us. I'm not sure what the relationship was nor how they'd managed to leave Russia at that particular time. All I knew was they were going to stay with my uncle Samuel and would pay a visit to our home.

I was sick with worry over how my father would treat them but I needn't have bothered.

He greeted them courteously if coolly, and for the rest of their visit he remained quite aloof. If he was as overawed by their presence and appearance as I was, his attitude is understandable.

They were two extremely tall men whose presence seemed to fill the room. They were probably years younger than I imagined them to be but with their ebony-black suits, matching three-quarter length coats, black brimmed hats and long, black beards they were a formidable sight.

My mother had prepared a lavish meal for our visitors yet, as we all sat round the table, I couldn't help feeling that, far from being a happy Jewish family reunion, the sombre atmosphere in the house was more conducive to a shivah – a ritual mourning.

Maybe they were as apprehensive of my father as I was of them. He ate in complete silence, an attitude which did nothing to ease the tension.

It was later, when the meal was finished and we were all sitting round the fire that they relaxed a little. For the next few hours we were enthralled with accounts of life in Russia. We heard of the vast, Siberian wastes; of dense forests; dancing bears and the intense cold.

We were horrified at the plight of Russian Jews and could hardly believe in the existence of pogroms: authorised, organised attacks on Jewish communities when they suffered arson, pillage, beatings, rape and often murder.

Throughout the evening, my father sat, taking all in but saying nothing. When the visitors were leaving, we waved them off with a tinge of regret and more than a little relief that the ordeal was over.

The time was drawing near for me to face another ordeal, my Barmitzvah, the most important event in a Jewish boy's life; the day he ceases to be a child.

This takes place on the first Shabbat after his thirteenth birthday when there is an impressive ceremony in the Synagogue followed by a grand coming of age party. From that day, in the eyes of all Jews, he is a grown man responsible for his own actions and destiny. He is capable of committing sin, is recognised as one of the minyan – the ten adult males required before a religious service can take place – and can also be called on to read the Torah in the Synagogue.

Lots of invitations were sent out and on the day, the Allerton Synagogue was packed with relatives and friends – all that is except my father.

This didn't upset me unduly. At least, if he showed no interest in my Barmitzvah he made no protest either. Quite the contrary, he offered to pick us up in the car later that night after the party which was being held at my uncle Joseph's house.

The long awaited November day dawned wet and bitterly cold. But as I set off for the service in my new, grey, pin-stripe suit, although still in short trousers, I was shaking more from nerves than the cold. My greatest worry was having to read the selected passage from the Prophets which was to be recited in Hebrew.

For weeks my mother, grandparents and brothers—especially Henry who was now a trainee rabbi—had coached me until I was word perfect. It wasn't unknown for the piece to be repeated parrot fashion with the narrator having no idea what he was saying. But not only could I recite it, to my great joy, I actually understood what it said.

Yet, on approaching the time when I would be standing on the bimah—the platform in the Synagogue—with only the chief rabbi beside me, I was filled with dread. There was nothing strange about that. Every novitiate experienced it but my case was slightly more harrowing. With the exception of my father my entire family always seemed more Jewish than me.

I had always taken pride in my two older brothers, Henry and David for playing their part in the war; Henry as a flying officer and David a rear gunner. And now that my future in the Jewish faith was assured, they seemed to be taking a great deal of interest in me. It was almost as if, for the first time, they saw me as their true brother.

After all the hours they and everyone else had spent on my tuition in readiness for this day my greatest fear was of letting them down.

Suddenly it was my turn to step up to the bimah. I felt self conscious wearing the gifts from my uncles Joseph and Samuel—my tefellin and tallith. Already these garments labelled me adult, yet I was sure a *man* shouldn't be quaking inside the way I was. The rabbi smiled kindly at me but my hand shook as he offered me the yad – the pointer used to avoid physical contact with the Torah.

As I glanced around the rows of encouragingly familiar faces, my nerves calmed a little. It wasn't a long passage to recite. Just a simple one from the book of the prophet Isaiah. Still, my mouth dried up and as I read aloud, the sounds didn't seem to be coming from me.

At last it was over. Again I looked along the lines of people and saw love shining in my grandpa Isaach's eyes; in my uncle Joseph's; uncle Samuel's and all my brothers. Up in the ladies' gallery, my mother, grandmother, sisters and all the others were smiling down at me; many with tear-filled eyes.

Congratulations abounded and at the party afterwards everyone was in jubilant mood. They had saved me from the world of a Gentile father. Even my mother was rejoicing openly but hers was not so much a victorious jubilation as one of relief. No more could *anyone* interfere in the way *she* conducted my life. From that day on, it belonged to me alone. There would never again be one single row over my spiritual future between her husband and herself.

Finally, after thirteen years, it seemed they could settle into a belatedly harmonious marriage.

That night, everyone was surprised when my father arrived at my party over an hour earlier than expected. He'd promised to pick us up but no one dreamed he would join the celebrations. Well, he didn't exactly *join in*, but it was nice to have him there.

Actually, our home life had been reasonably serene for months as my father accepted my coming Barmitzvah graciously. Perhaps even he was partly relieved that responsibility for his son was drawing to an end.

Of course, the volatile nature my parents shared never quietened down completely but from the day of my

Barmitzvah their squabbles could never be about me. I noticed another difference too. My father would deliberately avoid a row and, whenever this wasn't possible, he would show much restraint during the argument *then* do everything in his power to restore the peace afterwards.

I attributed this change to his war experiences and to my newly acquired adult status but realise now, it was because of mother's delicate health. By this time, added to the diabetes, she was also suffering from tuberculosis. But *man* or not, I knew nothing about it. I did know she was terrified of hospitals and often heard her beg my father never to let her go into one. He was so tender with her at those times and always gave his word that he never would.

When I was fourteen, I left school to take up an engineering apprenticeship. Our home life seemed to improve every day and life was never kinder.

That year father suggested taking us to Scotland to visit his relatives. I'd met my paternal grandparents in the past but this holiday would give us all the opportunity of getting to know each other better. As proof of the improvement in my maternal family relationships, Charlie, Aida and her husband were also going with us.

On a gloriously bright July day, accompanied by our alsatian, Rinty, we set off for Glasgow in our brand new grey Standard Vanguard and, as a family, we had never been so united or as happy.

In pre-motorway days, the journey to Scotland took far longer than today so, en route, we spent the night camping in a farmer's field where we had a terrifying experience.

With the portable camping-light still on, we were all just bedding down when, silhouetted in shadow on the tent wall, we saw the most horrendous apparition. A huge monster, easily ten feet tall, stood with tongue fully extended and emitting fiendish sounds. I let out a shriek and Rinty leapt to his feet growling, the hackles on the back of his neck standing inches high.

Every horror film I'd ever seen came to the fore of my mind and I could hardly believe it when my father said he would go out to investigate. Much as I applauded his bravery, I feared for his safety and on hearing him making equally strange sounds I knew we were all doomed.

Within seconds, he returned to the sanctuary of our canvas shelter, quite unharmed but convulsed with laughter. The fiend turned out to be the farmer's sheep-dog magnified many times in the shadows thrown from our lamp. He was so resentful of our alsatian's presence on his territory, under cover of darkness he'd come to issue some canine threats.

On reaching Glasgow we all stayed with my grandparents and in the following days we toured the area and met many more hitherto, unknown relatives. It was a wonderful holiday and at the end of two weeks, with the promise of a return visit the following year, we set off for home in beautiful weather. The intense heat was unsuitable for my mother but being young I barely noticed her discomfort.

Again we camped overnight and arrived back in Liverpool the following morning – the Shabbat.

My mother was absolutely worn out and went straight up to bed. It had been a tiring journey for us all and I believed a good rest was all she needed. It was some time later when my father became very agitated and sent for uncle Joseph that I realised she was suffering from more than exhaustion. There had been times when, due to her refusal to either consult a doctor or to take insulin, she'd lapsed into a coma and I was afraid this was what was happening again.

As she lay in the bed I noticed for the first time how, for a woman of her size, she looked remarkably frail. It must have been the shock of this discovery that deafened me to my father's pleas to bring her a fresh glass of water. When his words eventually registered, I dashed downstairs to get it and raced back to her room.

My father was cradling her in his arms and I barely made

out what she was saying to him, 'As man proposes . . . so God disposes . . . of all the plans you and I have made. It is going to end like this.'

As I moved closer to the bed to give her the glass of water my father turned to look at me. He didn't speak. He couldn't speak. I sensed his inward struggle to fight back the tears as he held her close; then I understood what his eyes were trying to convey. My mother was dead – lost to us both.

An overwhelming numbness gripped my emotions but my body responded to instruction. Without a word or a tear I walked from the room and from the house. For a while I stood at the gate until uncle Joseph came and stood beside me. It fell to him to go and tell grandma and grandpa that Aida, their daughter, always affectionately known to them as Chuckles, had died and I went with him.

My brother, Henry, the young rabbi, was the first to recover his senses and took complete charge of everything. My father was reduced to some kind of stupor and seemed grateful to have the responsibility lifted from him. In my abject misery, only one thing brought me close to tears. It was when my grandfather showed great sympathy to my father and placed his arm around his shoulders.

Perhaps if my young mind had been given time to absorb what had happened, I may have reacted differently. But there was no time.

Within an hour of my mother's death the house was teeming with people for the Shivah. This is when the entire family and friends gather together to watch over and pray for the deceased.

In accordance with custom, my mother was clothed in a simple, white linen gown and was lying in a very plain coffin, unadorned in any way.

The whole proceedings were quite incomprehensible to me. Only that morning we'd arrived home from our unforgettable holiday. I'd never known such happiness as over the past two weeks – and now? Now the world was turned upside down.

In a sense I envied all those around me for showing such practical qualities at this time. And I couldn't help noticing my father wasn't amongst them. He moved about like a zombie being told what to do and how to do it. People had to think for him and if there were ever any doubts in their minds about the love my parents held for each other, they must surely have been dispelled in those dreadful hours following her death.

In the hot, middle-eastern climate the dead are always placed beneath the ground as soon as possible. This practice is still followed by Jews no matter where in the world they live and, in true Hebrew tradition, my mother's funeral was to take place on the day following her death, the cortege leaving from her parents' home.

It was one of those heavy, threatening days when it is very hot and a storm seems imminent. There was just the hearse and a string of private cars to convey the four bearers and the other mourners. No women are allowed to attend Jewish funerals and there were no flowers in the Allerton Synagogue where we gathered for the prayers.

The interment was in the Jewish cemetery – Bet Hahayyim, House of Life – in the Liverpool suburb of Broad Green.

4: Rebellious Years

I had said 'goodbye' to my mother and only now was I fully aware of the tremendous influence she'd exercised in everyone's life. But there were still no tears from me. Quite the contrary. In place of sorrow there was an alien bitterness in my heart. I felt cheated.

There was resentment against my brothers and sisters for having so much of *my* mother's time and love before I was born.

My mind dwelled on all the controversy between my parents and grandparents during my fourteen years of life and of how she had skilfully sustained the very fragile peace between my father and the rest of the family.

But most of all there was a mounting anger at God for robbing me of her love just at the time when I was most confident of a happy future and therefore at my most vulnerable.

My father had loved my mother deeply and simply couldn't cope with her loss. Whereas a Torah-obedient Jew would observe the ritual mourning, he quickly broke under the strain and immediately after the funeral sought solace in drink. I was an encumbrance in the house and barely received a kind word from him. There was only one solution for my present problem – to leave home and move in with my grandparents.

My stay lasted for two weeks during which time, I tried to exercise my adultness by going out with some friends and taking my first strong drink. Nearly fifteen years old, I was under age but this merely added piquancy to the adventure – one that backfired on me when I arrived home.

My grandparents had already retired and in the dark I stealthily, if unsteadily crept up to bed only to encounter, part way up the stairs, two blazing red staring eyes on a level with my own.

My shriek of terror brought grandpa Isaach and grandma Aida running from their bed. The light was switched on and I was relieved to discover it was not the dreaded 'D.T.s' I was suffering from but the curiosity of a trespassing cat. Nevertheless, it was hours before I was allowed to go to my bed as grandpa insisted on reading the household riot act from start to finish. Needless to say, my taste for alcohol diminished for quite a while after that night.

By now the rest of the family were all gone their separate ways to lead pious lives within the community leaving me to feel totally isolated. And it was at this time just when I needed it most that my eldest brother, Henry, came forward. At thirty-two, besides being a respected rabbi, he was also a shrewd businessman and offered to help me forge my future. Alas it seemed the only assets I possessed were a lively imagination and some very hard lessons in life taught me by my grandpa.

I felt a slight indignation at first. Was it a genuine desire to help his young half-brother or was it rather to help protect the family honour which that young brother threatened to bring into disrepute? However, I talked over with him a business scheme that had been in my mind for a long time. It was no more than a pipe dream still, discussing it would serve to prove to Henry that there was an element of ambition and stability in my make-up.

There was some old property in the north of the city which showed great potential for conversion to flats. For a deposit of £50 and a mortgage payment of £1 per week it was a bargain. The snag was that any prospective buyer would need capital for the conversion.

Henry listened patiently and to my astonishment, said he would like to view the property.

He was quite impressed both with it and with his young brother's foresight and astonished me even more by offering a loan of £700 to start me up in business. At fifteen years of age, I must have been the youngest property tycoon in the city and was determined to make a success of the venture.

There were eleven rooms one of which was hastily adapted for my own living accommodation. The rest would take a tremendous amount of labour to restore them to anything like the standard I had in mind. Fortunately, my engineering colleagues knew several people who were either apprenticed or already qualified in all the necessary trades and they were all looking for work.

From then on, in addition to my engineering studies and homework, my evenings and weekends were dedicated to the building renovations.

But over the next four years as I plunged myself into the work, maybe due to fatigue, I began for the first time to miss having the love and warmth of my family around me.

Soon after leaving home I frequently called on my father but he would be drunk and in drink he was unsociable and ill-tempered so the visits grew fewer.

None of my relatives ever visited me with the exception of Henry who was now more business adviser than loving brother and it was love that I longed for – especially my mother's. I became even more bitter than in the first few days after her death and at last, tears which refused to flow then overwhelmed me but they did little to bring relief. I felt ashamed of my emotions. At thirteen I had supposedly become a fully-fledged adult. Yet, at seventeen, inside I felt like an abandoned child.

It is often under such circumstances, when one is bereft of loving support, and consumed with self-pity and bitterness that Satan moves in to take over where human kindness has failed.

Liverpool was no different from any other city around the world. Beneath its facade of bright lights and respectable appearance lay a jungle seething with crime, violence, dirt and corruption; an environment in which you either learned to take care of yourself or fell victim to its darker side. I chose the former. By day I too hid under a facade of respectability. By night I adopted a very different role, one completely alien to my days of the Torah, Talmud and Synagogue teaching.

And the course which took me into this sinister underworld came about quite by accident.

It was a miserable, rain-swept March day. I should have been attending the technical college but the urge to skip classes was too great. I'd arranged to meet a girl later that evening and decided to idle the waiting time in the city centre.

Over the years, the dance-halls, clubs and pubs had grown as familiar to me as my own back-yard at the flats. Strangely enough, although I smoked, despite the seedy places I frequented, I wasn't a heavy drinker. Perhaps that first experience was still with me. That particular day was spent wandering in and out of the many establishments; having a chat here, a game of snooker there and by tea-time, hunger was making itself evident so I made my way to a good Chinese restaurant opposite the Grafton dancehall.

The place was empty although the cluster of white-coated waiters busily yet quietly occupied suggested that there was a full house. The only sound was of soft, oriental music coming through the concealed speakers.

As Kosher no longer figured in my menu, I ordered a meal of my personal choice and was halfway through the soup when a gang of about six lads barged in through the door like a charging herd of elephants. They were using the foulest language and the stench of alcohol from their breath and clothes almost choked me.

On entering they immediately fell into a clowning

routine, throwing cruet pieces and food morsels from an uncleared table. I decided this didn't concern me until a piece of brown bread crust landed right in the middle of my soup. They burst out laughing and trying to keep calm I looked up and said, 'Hey, let that be the last one.'

The first two came towards me, describing in detail just how they were going to divide my body up. My muscles tightened and I knew it was either them or me. My clenched fist shot out like a power hammer to catch the first attacker under his chin. I was so surprised at my hitherto unsuspected physical power that I bent down to check if he was all right. At that precise moment, a second assailant moved forward to tower over my stooped form and took the full force of my head as I straightened up again!

The impact was shattering and its sound echoed all round the place blotting out the soothing notes emitting from the speakers. In total amazement I surveyed the once peaceful restaurant. With both my attackers nursing their wounds, tables overturned and the white tablecloths displaying red blotches of blood and spilled tomato soup it resembled a mini battlefield.

Terrified and convinced I'd reacted too strongly I braced myself to take on their four friends who were sure to wreak vengeance. But they didn't. Instead, with hands held high, they asked my permission to leave; a request I was pleased to grant.

The restaurant was quickly restored to normality and I resumed my meal. On going to settle my account later, the young Chinese manager refused to accept my money. In fact he handed me five £1 notes and thanked me profusely for stopping the disturbance.

Speechless I gaped at him for a while then pocketing the reward I left the restaurant shaking my head in disbelief.

All that evening I mulled over the incident and told friends about it. Simply by giving a bit of protection I'd earned £5. There was clearly prospect of riches in such actions. Not that I was in need of money. Grandpa Isaach had taught me well. Perhaps too well. Profitable though my business was, I wanted more and this seemed an easy way of getting it.

My reputation for self defence – interpreted by some as a penchant for violence – soon spread, especially around my less salubrious haunts. People were latching on to me; the type of people needed for the business I had in mind.

There were twenty-seven on the 'staff' and after a lengthy period of planning we formed ourselves into a protection business. We found an open market in the city's plush restaurants, cafés, clubs and dancehalls owned mostly by Chinese and blacks and the money soon rolled in. It gave me security and the more cash that came my way the better I felt. It was becoming my god.

I kept up my studies and used every spare moment to arrange my 'staff'.

In the beginning no one refused our services but eventually, as was expected, the protected ones began to rebel. This was when we went into action, threatening and often resorting to violence. Any clients who balked at paying their dues would have furniture and windows smashed. Naturally, this did little to encourage business for them. No one wanted to spend an evening in an establishment where violence was likely to erupt at any moment. The defaulters rarely needed any further persuasion to pay up.

With an operation like ours, the rewards were good but there were hazards to contend with. Our success attracted the jealous attention of rival gangs who wanted to step into our little enterprise and take over. There were some bitter conflicts with these people. In one of these incidents my nose was broken. In another I was stabbed.

At this particular time I had been in the property business for three years and had just sold my first block of flats for £2,700; a very good profit. For £2,000 I bought a second run-down tenement and proceeded to renovate that to the same standard as the previous one. I sold this one four years later for £4,700 – another great profit.

However, at that stage, at the age of twenty-one, I was called on to do my duty for Queen and country within the National Service for two years.

As my army training was done at Catterick camp in Yorkshire I was able to get home to Liverpool most weekends. Later, while serving abroad, a senior member of the 'staff' took my place.

This was the time of the Korean war and it was to that small spot on the globe that I was posted as soon as my training was over. Danger lurked constantly and the oriental jungle in no way resembled the comparative peace of the city jungle which was home. However my army days were short-lived.

Making our silent way through the humid terrain one day, we were ambushed by an American army patrol that mistook us for the enemy. Experience taught all troops not to hesitate before shooting. The US patrol aimed, fired and hurled grenades in our direction. The soldier immediately in front of me was killed instantly. At first I thought I was uninjured. Next I heard 'They're Limeys!' Then a loud buzzing followed by agonising pain in my head and ears told me I hadn't escaped completely. I awoke in the hospital to be informed I was suffering from shock, concussion and that my hearing was permanently damaged.

Within weeks I was medically discharged and on my way home. My National Service had lasted precisely thirteen months of the expected two years.

It wasn't long before I returned to my peacetime work in Liverpool and it wasn't long before my nose was broken again in the course of a rival dispute. No sooner was I recovered from that blow when someone used a length of steel scaffolding on it.

The Chinese doctor was very polite but told me in no uncertain terms that if any more damage was done to my nose, not only would he be unable to restore its shape, I could develop serious health and breathing problems in my later years. I was almost twenty-five at the time and although my dotage seemed an infinity away this ominous threat, added to my permanent deafness in one ear, forced me to review my whole life.

For some while my activities had been catching the attention of the police who always seemed to be in evidence wherever my 'staff' and I were. I lived off organised violence and was happy to go on doing so but not if it meant involvement with the police. They made me feel uncomfortable about my lifestyle.

One incident did very little to appease my conscience. I met up with my brother Henry, who asked me whether I'd ever heard about 'this mad Jew' with the terrible reputation whom everyone was talking about. He never realised that 'this mad Jew' was none other than his own younger brother!

The crucial point came one evening when some of my friends had been summonsed for loitering on a corner. It was a ruse meant as a warning and we knew it. Out of bravado I attended the court proceedings. After the case had ended and I was making my way down the impressive staircase in the lofty Victorian building, I was stopped by a detective-sergeant. He was a big man and the menacing look in his eyes said he knew all there was to know about me. I felt myself shrinking inside and wanted to run but his gaze held mine and I stood my ground.

He glared at my expensive gold watch and rings. Where did I get all my money from, he asked.

I explained that I was a Jew from a wealthy family. 'Don't all Jews have money?' I asked in a light-hearted manner. It was lost on him.

'Who do you hang around with?' he asked, and referring to the loiterers in court, 'How do *you* come to know these lads?'

These questions were simple to answer. The one that had me stammering was 'How do you keep ending up in the hospital casualty ward?'

If my attempt at humour had been lost on him, *my* consternation at this point didn't escape his notice. How could he know about that? Was I under surveillance? That must be the most stupid question I'd ever asked myself. The answer was self-evident. Hadn't we all suspected it for long enough and wasn't this whole incident of the loitering charge nothing more than official chicanery?

He would have me 'put away' if I didn't watch my step was his parting threat and it wasn't an idle one. It was 1960. So far I had done nothing worthwhile with my life and whether it was from fear of the law or a maturing outlook I decided the time had come to get out of the business.

5: God of Abraham, Isaach and Jacob

In my determination to change my ways and earn an honest living, the first consideration was to resume my engineering studies. Strangely, no sooner did I embark upon this than I found obtaining my degree became the most important thing in my world.

Meanwhile, I needed to find work and with my reputation it soon came my way—on the fringe of the underworld. I secured an evening job as 'bouncer' in a city club and, second to leaving my life of crime, it turned out to be the best move I ever made.

This came about one evening when a group of teenage girls seated at a table near the stage were getting a bit over exuberant. Their chatter and loud shrieks of merriment were disturbing the other patrons and I walked over to ask if they would keep the noise down. When one of them remonstrated with me for interfering, my temper began to rise and I pointed a threatening finger at her saying she would be thrown out if she didn't behave. But when I found myself gazing into a pair of deep, dark eyes and my concentration wavered for an instant; just long enough to give her the advantage. She quickly grabbed an empty Coke bottle from the table and thrust the neck of it over my outstretched finger.

For a moment I stared at it then glared angrily at the girl. Her eyes were laughing into mine. Her friends were tittering so were the people at the surrounding tables. The ludicrous sight of the bottle hanging on my finger was too much and I too dissolved in a fit of laughter.

The culprit wore a skirt and top which accentuated her height and slender figure giving an extraordinary poise to someone of her years. Her hair was dark and cut in a short, fashionable style. I thought her make-up was overdone but those eyes were riveting.

Every spare moment of that evening, I wandered across to the table to talk to her and with every passing moment I liked her more. She told me she was eighteen was a shorthand typist and lived with her parents in the Old Swan area of Liverpool.

When it was time for the club to close and I watched her tugging on her black and grey check coat, and preparing to leave with her friends, I felt a sudden panic. Supposing she didn't come to the club again. This could be the one and only time we would meet. Something must be done about it. She couldn't simply walk out of my life like that. Where the courage came from to make me go and ask if I could take her home I don't know. And at first I thought I'd misheard when she said 'Yes'. But I hadn't.

It wasn't a very romantic journey to her home in the back of a friend's open van on that freezing, snowy night. Still it gave us cause for many more laughs and we discovered we had a lot in common.

After some weeks of doing reputable work, apart from my engineering studies, respectability was beginning to pale a bit and sometimes I'd actually found myself longing for the old days of the 'staff'; big money, risk and adventure. Jackie was my salvation. It was only her guidance and wisdom that kept me from slipping back into crime – perhaps to end up in jail or a hospital morgue. My family had completely abandoned me and she brought into my life what had been missing for years – love and a sense of belonging.

Ironically, it was also Jackie who was responsible for my family remembering my existence. On learning I had a

Gentile girlfriend they began to make repeated visits to my home, begging me to end the relationship.

Their pleas went unheard and Jackie and I went on as before. All her family accepted my Jewish background although they were opposed to my reputation. Well, that was no problem. I was now a changed character. I gained my degree; sold the second block of flats at a good profit and we seemed headed for a secure future.

After three years, we decided it was time to really settle down and Henry was the first of my family to be told. Naively, I had a notion he might even marry us in his Synagogue. He flatly refused and word of the forthcoming marriage spread around the Jewish community like wildfire. Again relatives, some I hardly knew, began visiting. The abuse and scorn poured out at me for wanting to *marry* a 'goy' was akin to an artillery barrage. 'God will punish you', 'Traitor!', 'No more a part of the family', 'Banned from the home' were some of the threats issued. I reminded myself, and them, that for the past few years of my life I'd been no part of the family.

When I went to tell my father he turned out to be my greatest opponent. 'You can't marry her. You are a Jew. She is a Gentile. It's not allowed,' he yelled.

I challenged him for a more logical reason. After all he had been a lapsed Jew who considered himself a Gentile, yet he'd married a Jewess – allowed or not. I seethed inside on remembering all the disharmony of my childhood for that very reason. Then he told me he'd promised my mother never to let me 'marry out'.

How could he have taken on such a promise, I wondered? If I was of marriageable age there was no question of him – or anyone else – *not letting me* 'marry out'.

My arguments were to no avail. Nor were his. We went ahead with our wedding plans, or as far as we could go, until we found someone who would marry us.

Jackie wanted a white wedding in church and being so in

love, I had almost forgotten how wide was the division between Jew and Gentile *outside* my own family. But it was soon brought back to me when we approached the first Anglican church in the Broad Green area of Liverpool.

The vicar, a slightly built man with dark-rimmed glasses and a receding hairline, was as blunt as some of my relatives had been. 'I'm sorry,' he said 'but you are not one of God's children!' His tone was of instant dismissal without even asking if I wanted to be one of his flock.

From there we went from church to church, searching for someone who would marry us. It was the same story each time. 'I'm sorry but you are a Jew', became the stock response. Eventually we believed it would have to be a registry office wedding and I knew Jackie was disappointed though she tried hard not to show it.

Then one warm, summer evening as we walked hand in hand along Green Lane, I spotted a Congregational church and asked Jackie 'Shall we try just once more?'

Tears brimmed in her eyes. 'It's no use,' she said '*They* won't marry us either.'

Nevertheless, I insisted on going through the procedure of asking and nearly fell through the floor when the minister said, 'Yes, I'll marry you.'

Then, sure he hadn't realised that I was a Jew, I took a deep breath and told him. Here it comes, I thought, steeling myself against his refusal.

'Ah, one of God's chosen people!' he exclaimed, 'That's no problem.'

Jackie and I gaped at him then looked at each other and smiled. We didn't dare stop smiling in case he changed his mind. He didn't. The wedding plans went ahead with us attending the church at intervals leading up to the big day for private talks about the sanctity of marriage.

For me the 'big day' was a whirl of white satin and red carnations; of white veil and red wine; black limousines and guests; speeches and wedding-cake.

At the marriage service I overcame my fear of Christians and their churches by keeping my eyes on my beautiful bride and my mind on the fact that, amongst her friends and relatives present, one of them was mine. My father came to our wedding.

Our honeymoon was spent in Jersey, from where we returned to set up home in a large, Victorian terraced house at Bootle, a Liverpool suburb.

However, married life turned out not to be the bed of roses we'd anticipated. Within a short time I became restive and I knew why. As a descendant from the line of Abraham, Isaach and Jacob, I was being made to suffer for 'marrying out'. My family considered me to be dead and completely ostracised me and out of sheer rebellion – with maybe a degree of malice – I was sorely tempted to return to my old way of life. By finally revealing myself as the 'mad Jew' they'd heard so much of in the past they would be given good reason for considering me *dead*; retribution indeed.

Conversely, I was no longer at liberty to make that choice. There was Jackie to consider and why should she be made to suffer through my wrongdoing? Together we talked over the situation and decided it would be in the best interest for all concerned if we moved right away from the city to make a completely fresh start elsewhere.

We moved to Ashton-in-Makerfield, a small mill town about fifteen miles from Liverpool, not too far from our home city and Jackie's family yet far enough from my family to give us peace.

Our new home was a modern bungalow in a semi-rural area; an ideal environment for rearing children and this became our next criterion, to start a family. But as time went on without any sign of a longed for child, again I began to hear the threats echoing in my mind 'Traitor' and 'God will punish you'. Could they have been right?

From old, staunch friends, reports were reaching me from Liverpool that our obvious infertility was a point of ridicule in my family. My sister, Aida, was actually quoted as saying 'It's a curse from God for marrying out'.

Evidently I wasn't the only one to think it.

Determined not to be childless, we eventually decided to adopt. Jackie was overjoyed at the prospect of becoming a mother and I hadn't the heart to disillusion her. It was general knowledge that to qualify as an adoptive parent one needed to be a superior specimen of mankind. I often wondered where all these *infallible* people came from and knew of many horror stories where those who did appear to be faultless were rejected on the flimsiest grounds. Once my character was delved into, it would prove to be extremely flawed. A lapsed Jew of dubious reputation.

Unbelievably, however, there wasn't a single hitch and in 1969 Simon arrived at our home. Aged three weeks, he'd never experienced life with anyone else and it was as though he were of our own flesh and blood right from the start.

Then three years later, Jackie returned from the doctor's one afternoon to announce that our recent suspicions were confirmed. To our astonishment and delight, she was pregnant. Some months later, on a glorious October evening in 1973, she gave birth to our daughter, Lesley.

Now with our two children we were a complete family — yet something was lacking. I grew restless again, maybe I had an inner longing for my family who had so cruelly cast me out. Deep inside of me there was a longing for something. Again Jackie and I discussed it and after much deliberation we felt it might solve everything if we took our little ones right away; somewhere where, in later years, malicious remarks and unkind curses couldn't reach them.

By now I had my engineering degree plus work experience. I was a young man with a wife and two young children; all the qualifications for emigration. On three separate occasions I applied for posts in South Africa, Canada and Australia and was offered all three. Three times we carried out all the necessary procedure for emigration to the respective countries and on each occasion, failed to go because some inner, nagging voice insisted that we stay.

But why? There was no reason to have any doubts or to reconsider our decision. We had overcome all the likely obstacles in lengthy discussions long before we took the first steps towards leaving the country. It was only because of *my* discontent that we'd decided to go in the first place. After all our preparations why should *I* suddenly feel we ought to stay?

During the period leading up to our emigration my wife had become involved in local activities – caring for old people and the like. After a few weeks when Mr and Mrs McDonald, two of our neighbours, invited her along to the local Baptist church, I didn't think it strange that she should go. It probably concerned the charity work she'd recently been doing, I thought. Only when she began to attend another, larger church in the same area did I take more notice. Something was happening to Jackie. There was nothing tangible or visible, she was simply *different*.

Jackie was always a happy girl and had often cheered me out of the doldrums. But now there was more than happiness in her. She positively radiated. Eventually I spoke to her about it and received a bigger shock than when she became pregnant as she told me, 'I have accepted Jesus as my personal saviour'.

Jesus? Jesus? The one responsible for so much persecution against my people and here was my own wife, accepting him into her life. Alarm bells rang in my head.

Of course Jackie had wanted a church wedding but this was largely due to it being an appropriate setting for the occasion; the fine clothes, flowers and photographs, rather than from some deep religious conviction.

Perhaps she believed in God. But *I believed in God*. It was Christianity that worried me. Christians were oppressors against my Jewish faith. I recalled stories of how the crusaders gave Jews the choice of believing and being baptised or being executed. And weren't they Christians who stood back while the Third Reich destroyed six million Jews? Some of my own family amongst them – and they were now Jackie's family, yet here she was going in complete opposition to everything she knew to be right. How could she?

Despite my horror I couldn't deny that love for this Jesus shone out through her eyes. Next she began taking the children to church each Sunday and I could hardly object when I had no alternative to offer them. My own religion had been sadly neglected in the past years.

Never once did Jackie suggest I accompany them yet I was so impressed by her being 'born again' as she called it, that one morning I resolved to go along to see for myself just what had brought about this change in her.

It was a fruitless visit. There was nothing special or particularly exciting that I could see so I simply signed the visitors' book and returned home. Well, if that's Christianity, I thought, they can keep it.

I had almost forgotten the incident when one day Jackie asked if I would mind a couple of the church people coming to see me. Out of courtesy to her I agreed. After all, I was a Jew. There was nothing *they* could tell me about the scriptures. The visit would be a history lesson for *them*.

The first one to come was a man named Alan Bridge. We had a lengthy chat and as he was leaving he offered me a copy of John's Gospel, reminding me that even John was a Jew. This was something I hadn't given a thought to until then. We bade farewell with me agreeing to see him again. Only this time I was determined, and would be prepared, to prove him wrong.

The Bible, as the Gentiles knew it, belonged to the Jews. Despite doing what he had, Jesus himself was a Jew. All those who wrote the Torah and Talmud were Jews. No, I would have no problems in proving them to be under a delusion. I could even afford to be generous by showing them where their beliefs were wrong. As for this John's Gospel, there were no such writings in the Torah.

I swallowed my pride and went to see my estranged brother, Henry. As a rabbi, he could tell me where to find the answers. He was so pleased at my renewed interest in the Hebrew faith he not only allowed me full use of the library in his own home, he also loaned me many books and charts. Had he known of my association with Gentiles my curiosity wouldn't have been so well received and he wouldn't have been so accommodating.

On arriving home, I spread the literature out but once the table was covered with books, papers and charts I was at a loss where to begin.

My first discovery was that John, the Jew, had spent a lot of time with Jesus, the carpenter's son from Nazareth.

In the New Testament book of Acts, I read where Gamaliel, a teacher of the law and much honoured man in the Sanhedrin, stood up and made a clear statement about the followers of Jesus, the Nazarene.

'Men of Israel,' he began, 'consider carefully what you intend to do with these men.' He went on to quote several incidents of men in the past who had claimed to come from God and later melted into oblivion. 'Leave these men alone! Let them go! For if their purpose or activity is of human origin, it will fail. But if it is of God, you will not be able to stop these men. You will only find yourselves fighting against God' Acts 5:34–39.

The more I read the more confused I became. No matter how I searched, my studies refused to reveal what I was looking for. Scripture after scripture was studied. Concealed somewhere within them was that which would prove beyond all doubt, Jesus was *not* the Messiah God had promised. Still the revelation I sought eluded me.

Finally, after much perusal, three options were left. Jesus was a fake. He was a fool or – he was who he claimed to be.

If he were either of the first two then he died for nothing.

That didn't make sense. No conman or fool would accept such torment as he had and suffer crucifixion when one word would release him from it all. There was absolutely no logic in such actions. Any charlatan or fool would have made good his escape even though he intended setting up business elsewhere. I was left with the third option. Jesus was who he said he was – the anointed one.

6: *The Yeshua Ha' Meshiach*

With the papers, charts, books and Bible still spread over the table I paced up and down the room, my thoughts spinning round. Chapter and verse were gone over again in my determination to ensure my intellect was better than that of any Gentile. All this achieved was that the web of intrigue developed even further with all the prophesies pointing towards Jesus Christ being the Yeshua Ha' Meshiach.

God had promised to send a saviour into the world; a Messiah who would be a light to all nations. But with the passing of time and no coming of the Messiah the earth became a principality of Satan where men worshipped false gods, idols and images.

In the midst of this heathen world my race, the Jews – descendants of Abraham – had waited patiently with hope and longing.

For centuries they lived as nomads in the land God had given them, learning and being moulded by him into a holy nation, a nation worthy of receiving the coming Messiah whom they were to offer as the ultimate sacrifice for all mankind.

Then two thousand years ago, a young man named Jesus, son of a carpenter from Nazareth, came out from the Judaean mountains claiming to be the promised one. Multitudes believed and followed him. Others were sceptical. They wanted a political saviour. One to free them from the yoke of the Roman Empire. When he did none of this and they cried for his blood and arranged his execution they were merely fulfilling the prophecies made generations before.

My thoughts were spinning. The whole object of my study was to confuse my Gentile visitors yet here I now was, in the ridiculous situation of questioning myself and all that had ever been taught me. The evidence for Jesus being the promised one was overwhelming.

I paced about some more until suddenly I fell to my knees, praying and begging the Yeshua to come into my heart.

Then I cried. As the tears of generations ran down my cheeks a heavy emotional burden drifted away from me and I grew aware that the Ruach Ha' Kodesh, the spirit of God, was in the room with me.

Slowly, I was reborn into the Holy Spirit of Jesus, the anointed one, and my life would never be the same again. Now I knew whose voice I had heard deep inside telling me not to leave the country. My life was destined for something else.

Nevertheless, although so much had been cleared up in my mind, there was something else to confuse me. If I had come to accept the Christian tenet what of my Jewishness?

I returned to check on my studies. Jesus was a Jew. The Bible was written by Jews. Indeed Paul had arranged his vast missionary duties to enable him to attend the feast of the Passover. Throughout his mission to the Gentile nations he couldn't stay away from the Synagogue. He circumcised Timothy although he had a Gentile father and in the first verse of his letter to the Romans he spoke quite openly of his Jewish origin.

Now the confusion was clearing. If I too was a Jew, and proud to be, yet I accepted Jesus as the Messiah, this could mean only one thing. I hadn't lost my Jewishness. It had been strengthened and I was now complete in the Yeshua Ha' Meshiach.

By Hebrew tradition any Jew who becomes a believer in

Christ is considered to be dead. It has been known in some Jewish homes to hold a funeral service for the offender. My relatives were steeped in their orthodox beliefs. If I was already dead to them for 'marrying out', now it would be worse. In their eyes I would *never even have existed.*

I don't know how my family reacted when they discovered what to them would be the iniquitous truth about me. For my part, I still loved them dearly and prayed God would some day take off their blinds to let them see their Messiah.

All my scheming had come to nought and when Alan Bridge called again, this time with a friend, Russ Fairhurst, it was to meet a very different Tom Sangster-Wilson. One who was spiritually re-born.

At Carnforth, about a hundred miles north of my home and bordering on the Lake District, there was a week long seminar due to take place at a Christian Bible College and Alan and Russ invited me to go.

After hearing their guest speaker, the renowned evangelist and Bible teacher, Charles Price, I would willingly have stood on a soap-box anywhere in the world to shout that God *had* sent the promised one in Jesus Christ.

However, the Lord had other plans for me.

One of my first resolutions on becoming a believer was to return to my old Liverpool haunts and make restitution with all those I'd preyed on in my mis-spent youth. Over the years, many had moved away from the area, leaving no trace of their whereabouts. Of those I did find, *not one* would accept reimbursement of any sort. And when I explained my reason for seeking them out, everyone wished me well for the future. I could only thank God and pray he would reimburse them for me in his own way.

After that week at the Bible College I told Alan and Russ it wasn't enough for *me* to discover that Jesus was the Messiah. I wanted to help spread the word of God; to tell people of my spiritual re-birth and help them find the Lord for themselves.

Alan and Russ soon found an opportunity for this. With them, I was to go into Garswood, a small village set in acres of plush farmland, close to Ashton-in-Makerfield where I lived and where, four hundred years ago, Protestant Puritans fought Royalist Catholics in Cromwell's England. There we would go from door to door, giving out Bible tracts, thus taking God to the people.

For a while this satisfied my longing but I soon realised, not even that was enough. God wanted more from me than simply knocking or ringing at people's doors. I discussed my frustrations with Alan and Russ and discovered these thoughts were mutual. Through us, the Lord had a lot to offer. It was for us to find a way of conveying it. And we did.

From the local council, we hired the village hall to hold our services but services of a very different kind from where a regimented congregation sat, knelt, and stood in a set ritual.

We had a new concept of what worship was all about. Our congregation would sit in a circle, all facing each other. They wouldn't simply be preached at and sermonised but would participate in the proceedings, praying as the spirit moved them and even offering confession if they wished. We called it The Calvary Christian Fellowship and met every Sunday.

We still kept up door-to-door visitation, gave Gospel messages and held evangelistic meetings in the hall.

The Holy Spirit was gaining strength within me. I was almost constantly praying, praising the Lord for coming into my heart. And it was during one of these sessions at home that I began to pray in strange tongues. Terror gripped me. Had some demon taken possession of my mind? In fear I ran all the way to a friend's house and spilled out my experience. They comforted me and showed me through the scripture that, rather than some malevolent spirit, it was the Holy Spirit. God had blessed me with one of his most precious gifts – one that many churches believe died at the time of Pentecost – I was praying with the tongues of angels.

When I first embarked on my Christian life it didn't occur to me that my Jewish background could ever be a drawback until I became aware of people wanting to make me into a *Gentile* Christian. That someone could be converted to Christianity was accepted. That someone could be converted to Christianity *and remain a Jew* was impossible.

It was so difficult trying to make them understand what were *blatant facts*. The followers of Jesus Christ and Jesus and his apostles were *all Jews*. They lived by the Old Testament – or Torah as we Jews know it. Didn't Jesus say 'I have not come to abolish the law but to fulfil it'?

Sometimes I despaired of ever being understood but I soldiered on. All those difficulties were just beginning to smooth out and everything was going well until one sunny Sunday morning as the service was drawing to a close. The Parish Hall door suddenly opened and in walked a uniformed policeman.

Had my past caught up with me? I'd been back to make my peace with my victims. What had I overlooked? Would the police understand I was a changed man, a believer?

How could I explain to someone who had come to arrest me that Jesus paid the price for all my sins when he died on the cross at Calvary?

PART II
THEN TO THE GENTILE

7: *The Iron Grip of the Church*

I was born in 1943 in the north west of England at St Helens, a large industrial town known as the glass producing centre of the world. At that time it lay under a mushroom of smoke from domestic coal-fires and within a ring of tall, puffing factory chimneys fuelled from well-stocked coal piles. All the smoke is gone now but the town still retains its proud glass manufacturing title.

My family was devout Roman Catholic and my home was in the parish of St Mary's, Lowe House, a beautiful Romanesque church affectionately called 'the poor man's cathedral'. From within those walls all the Catholics of the parish were watched over constantly by its strict order of Jesuit priests.

The church school stood alongside this bastion of orthodox Catholicism and the eyes of the patriarchal parish priest were on every pupil's religious and secular education. Even their after-school activities came under scrutiny.

My mother, Annie, a plump, fair haired woman who stood a little under five feet in height and spoke with a broad Lancashire accent was totally absorbed in her religion.

Often she quoted 'Jesus was the very first Catholic who ordained that Peter be the second Catholic and the first pope. Doesn't it say in the Bible "You are Peter and on this rock I will build my church and the gates of hell shall not overcome it"?'

I will never forget the times I wanted to play with non-Catholic children.

'Can I play with Tommy?' I would ask.

'What church does he go to?' would be her response.

If the children were Church of England they would just about be tolerated although even then, I could tell from the look in her eyes, she was uncertain. There was a chance the priest could be on his rounds.

Only C of E believers were considered fit to mix with as, in my mother's view, none other than RCs or C of E's could possibly be Christians.

Nevertheless, as a family she believed we were obliged to show them all Christian love.

In the adoring eyes of my mother, I was growing into a good Catholic boy and she was thrilled that both her sons were serving on the altar. Her attitude towards this was like the story of Hannah and Samuel – 'God gave them to me and he can have them back'.

I used to regret that our home circumstances didn't match the splendours of our religious life.

My maternal grandmother had been born in the local workhouse. We were poor, and never knew where the next meal or even the next penny was coming from. And although we lived in a big terraced house in the 'posh' part of town that was as near as we ever got to opulence.

The house had a parlour, living room and kitchen downstairs. Upstairs was a bathroom – minus running hot water – and four bedrooms. But with ten people living there even the parlour was utilised as a bedroom.

Father and mother had one room. Grandmother and grandfather another. In the parlour slept my great-grandmother and a cousin while I shared a bed with my older brother, Joe, in the same room as great-aunt Jane and her husband, 'mad uncle Bob'.

In winter the only form of heating came from a makeshift hot water bottle – a warmed-up house brick wrapped in a shawl – and from the glow of the interior gas lamps. Electricity was for those who could afford it.

My mother's uncle by marriage, 'mad uncle Bob', a black-haired, swarthy skinned man was just over four feet tall in his stockinged feet. However, what he lacked in size he made up for in other ways. It was his name which was entered in the rent book and he often made it quite plain to everyone – especially after a night at the local pub – that we were mere lodgers to be at his beck and call.

The overcrowded household was, however, something we had chosen. My father had once been offered a colliery employee's house but refused it on the grounds that it was too small for the *entire* family who preferred to stay together.

Although the Second World War had come and gone, my male relatives still retained some Victorian standards. They tipped their hats to ladies and gave up their seats on public transport. Alas, they also hung on to some other less commendable Victorian attitudes when they spent almost all their wages in trying to drink local public houses dry.

Friday nights were a ritual. My father, grandfather and uncle Bob would come home from working in the mine covered from head to foot in thick, black coal-dust. They would each take their turn in stripping off their clothes, shaving and taking a bath in the metal tub placed in front of a roaring fire, made up for their benefit. This was followed by climbing into their best suits, having fish and chip teas then jogging off to the pub, talking, joking and laughing all the way.

As a child I could never understand how strong drink could change a person's character the way it did my relatives' – and within so short a time. But on their return, the red alcoholic glare in their eyes told me they were ready to pick a fight with anyone at the slightest provocation.

Many's the time I was forced to crawl under the

sideboard when, in one of his drunken fits, mad uncle Bob would grab a carving knife and make a lunge at someone. Then, without a care as to where we would spend the night, he would further enforce his authority by demanding that we all leave his premises. By the following morning when he had sobered up, overwhelmed by remorse, *we* would be forgiven for our bad behaviour!

This continued throughout my childhood and not once did anyone consider calling the police. I can only believe it was the strength of the family bond which prevented this.

My father, Harold, was fair-skinned but had dark hair which was grey before he reached middle-age. He was almost six feet tall and well built; qualities which, in his younger days, secured him a place in the forward line of a local Rugby League team. Yet despite his size and strength, when sober, he was a very placid natured man.

I well recall the day my school attended a lunchtime church service and Latin lesson – the language of the Roman Catholic church – and I decided to skip both. When my father heard of it, for the one and only time in his life, he put me over his knee to give me a hiding. That episode did wonders for my Latin but not, alas, for much else in my education.

At the age of fifteen when I finished school, although I was able to recite lengthy portions of Latin, I could barely read or write.

'Oh, he'll do for the pit,' said mad uncle Bob.

'May even do for the army,' said another relative.

Well, I was rather ambitious and that last remark triggered off ideas which had been lurking in the back of my mind. Although the RAF was out – I felt they were too posh – for some time I'd dreamed of joining either the army or the navy.

The ink on my employment card was still wet when I jumped on board a bus for the hour long journey to Liverpool and its London Road recruiting office.

The sergeant at the front desk was massive. He had an enormous ginger moustache and an Irish Guards badge smack in the centre of his peak cap. 'Right, me boy,' he said in a thick Irish brogue, 'so you want to be a soldier!'

'Yes, s . . sir,' I stammered, intimidated by the sheer bulk of him. Unmoved by my obvious nervousness he went on, 'Well, there'll be just the test to do, then we can get your parents' consent.' He stooped low to peer into my eyes concluding with 'And we'll be 'aving you in.'

That finished it. I hadn't expected to have a test of any sort. I'd always believed soldiering consisted of little more than pointing a rifle in the right direction and knowing how to fire the thing. As for 'parents' consent', well, I hadn't shared my plans with anyone at home so it had never occurred to me I would need anyone's consent. It was *my* life, wasn't it?

The written test took only a short while and from the expression on the sergeant's face I knew this was the only time he'd had a completely blank sheet of paper handed in. In his eyes I read the question 'Don't you know *anything*?' What he actually said was 'Try again when you're a bit older son. And try a bit of schooling as well.'

Feeling useless and in the dumps, I returned home, my head hanging in shame. After I'd spilled my heart out to my mother she simply smiled and said, 'Ah, well, Bobbie, perhaps it isn't for you.'

For the next year or so I wandered aimlessly from job to job; helping a coffin-maker in one, working at a dry cleaners in another, then, as an apprentice, slapping plaster on to walls. It was as though I was searching for a place to settle, belonged nowhere and no one wanted me.

At thirteen I'd given up serving on the altar. To please my mother I still attended church but my spiritual life was gradually slipping into the background. Evenings were taken up with girlfriends, betting offices and wandering into the town centre bars, drinking long before I'd reached the legal age.

Then one day when I should have been busy at my work, plastering, but was actually leaning out of a window watching the world go by, I suddenly remembered my old ambition. Over the two years since leaving school I'd gleaned a bit of education. It wasn't much but it would possibly suffice to get me through the test I'd failed the first time round. And at seventeen I was old enough to have another go at enlisting without needing anyone's consent.

The following morning, instead of going to work, I went back to the recruiting office in Liverpool.

This time the sergeant, a younger, much smaller and less formidable man didn't bother to tell me my test results. Still, they must have proved satisfactory because he talked me into joining his own regiment – The First Lancashire Regiment Prince Of Wales Volunteers.

Delighted at this, without asking any questions on what an army career entailed, I signed on for six years was given my enlistment date and walked from the office clutching in my hand the 'King's Shilling' – a tradition dating from when a recruit was given a day's wage for signing on.

My mother was terribly upset at what I'd done yet she was quite philosophical about it. It would get me away from all the family disputes and provide me with opportunities for travel and status I could never hope to have otherwise.

8: *The King's Shilling*

December, 1960, saw me sworn into the army and stationed about thirty miles from home at Preston in Fulwood Barracks – a quadrangle of tall, drab, rectangular buildings. Army life was not going to be the glamorous vocation I'd daydreamed about from boyhood.

Our drill sergeant was a veteran of every sort of campaign from fighting in the jungles of Malaya to clearing out the NAAFI at Aldershot. For the moment he was applying his know-how and personal brand of toughness to a bunch of raw recruits.

Nevertheless, as he barked out the orders and we marched up and down the square, it seemed to my untrained eye we would never be sufficiently proficient to be called on to perform ceremonial duties at Buckingham Palace, such as Trooping the Colour. Still, it was only our first week of service.

Of course our six weeks basic training involved far more than 'square bashing'. We had PT and inspections. There was unarmed combat when we learned how to slit a throat 'in one easy go'. We were also taught how to blast someone to oblivion with a machine-gun. From reveille to lights out we were kept on the go.

Stationed at Preston meant I was able to get home for the first two weekends. On the Monday of our third week, the platoon sergeant warned us 'In the army we work hard and play hard'. Taking him at his word, for the rest of that week we worked like slaves in the naive belief we would get another free weekend. But Saturday morning saw us brushing the parade ground, collecting litter bins and polishing the cookhouse windows. It was lunchtime when we were rewarded for all our endeavours by being given the rest of the day off. The joy was short-lived though. We were not allowed to go out of the camp and so had to spend the evening in the NAAFI – every serviceman's supermarket, restaurant and licensed bar.

There was one consolation in not going home though. I wouldn't need to go to mass the following morning.

Our NAAFI resembled one of those ancient church halls found tucked away down dark, side streets. However, the buxom blonde serving behind the counter was quite partial to men with fat wallets. Anyone displaying affluence could be her escort home at the end of the night. Well, that let me out so I settled for half a dozen bottles of brown ale.

I awoke the following morning to strong shafts of light piercing the highly polished windows and a voice echoing down the long corridor, 'Church parade in five minutes. Out of your bunks, *now*.'

I had forgotten they had 'church parade' in the army and leapt out of bed, took a two second wash and was half way down the stone steps before it struck me, I had a massive hangover from the previous night.

The bright sunlight and the duty NCO shouting 'RC's on the right. C of E's on the left,' didn't help one bit.

'What if you're neither?' a lad from Liverpool shouted.

'Cookhouse party' came the instant reply.

The lad quickly chose a religion and jumped into line with the rest of us.

There was something else I soon learned – army pay didn't go far so to earn extra money, I signed on for a further three years. At seventeen there seemed little difference in six and nine years.

As time passed we were gradually eased out of our civilian state and into an ordered army routine. Soon we were a platoon of tough fighting men ready to face anything. Or so we thought.

One morning on parade the platoon sergeant called everyone to attention and gave the command, 'By the right, quick march! Get your arms swinging. You're marching like a load of drunken ducks.'

'Where are we going, sergeant?' someone ventured to ask.

'A boxing tournament' was the answer accompanied by a look which implied 'And no more questions'.

However, when we arrived at the gym it turned out not to be the sort of boxing match we'd anticipated. We weren't to be the spectators but were each given a set of oversized gloves then ordered to belt the living daylights out of each other for five minutes or until we dropped on the mat. This barbaric ritual, we were informed, was to induce aggression and complete our dehumanising.

At the end of that bout there were more bloody noses and cut lips than I had ever seen in my local church boxing club. And the exercise was successful.

Aggression had been induced and I was going to assert myself. That weekend I was due for some leave but *home* meant going to confession and mass. I didn't want that. At forty-three years of age my mother was pregnant again and in her condition I wouldn't have upset her by going home but refusing to attend church. So, on reaching St Helens, instead of going to see my parents, I went to spend my weekend leave at a friend's home. It was time to start on those deadly sins.

Returning to camp on the Sunday night I had a feeling of great satisfaction. The fact I had broken some of the Ten Commandments, one of them being 'Honour thy father and thy mother' didn't matter at all.

During the latter stages of our training, life was one long miserable round of initiative and self survival exercises with our tired, aching bodies often cold, wet and mud splattered and our feet covered in raw blisters.

But at last it was over. From out of a bunch of immature, nervous adolescents had emerged confident, physically fit young men.

The toil, sweat, tears – and the laughter – had all been swallowed up in time. All that remained was the passing out parade followed by fourteen days embarkation leave before being posted to the British Army on the Rhine. And all for a King's Shilling.

My mental image of the Fatherland was of brass bands, beer festivals, romantic trips along the Rhine and of course – war. This conjured up another picture of fair young men, gleaming jackboots and choruses of 'Sieg Heil!'

But just as in the case of army life, Germany was not what I'd expected.

St David's Barracks lay in the suburbs of Hilden, a small industrial town. The camp itself was an accumulation of brick buildings well concealed from public view by tall evergreen trees.

This was to be home for the next two and a half years during which we would be custodians of world peace facing the might of the Red Army.

During my spell in Germany I learned to drive, then took medical training to become the Regimental Medical Assistant.

But within a very short time, the attraction of the responsibility of protecting the western world from communism wore off. I'd joined the army to see the world but so far the world was proving to be an extremely dull place.

Boredom was relieved only by visits to the camp cinema and NAAFI or the beer bars and brothels of Dusseldorf's red light district. Satan must have been very proud of his latest recruit.

After the allotted time, the regiment was posted back to Britain. This time to Catterick on the bleak Yorkshire moors but for only a brief stay before we were boarding a plane to whisk us off to the tiny kingdom of Swaziland in south east Africa.

Again my hopes for the exotic were dashed when we arrived at our camp; rows of squat, asbestos huts surrounded by a high wire fence in the most barren area imaginable.

There our routine was made up of military exercises and controlling an outbreak of foot and mouth infection the civil authorities simply couldn't cope with.

Consequently the novelty of Africa soon began to pale. Once again, solace was found in the camp beer with its ensuing hangover or visits to the local town where one had an even chance of contacting gonorrhea or syphilis.

How I cursed the army – myself even more – for yielding to its promise of glory, danger and excitement.

Even on that searingly hot June day as I was walking past the company office I was mulling over in my mind all that lay ahead of me – or rather all the empty uneventful years stretching ahead of me – when I heard the sergeant major roaring 'Carroll, get yourself over to the adjutant's office, on the double.' I'd been considering a lengthy NAAFI break but when he used that tone, he meant *on the double*. In the short time it took to reach battalion headquarter all sorts of things raced through my mind. Why me? What had I done?

The door was slightly ajar and in response to my timid knock the adjutant invited me in. At first he avoided looking at me as I stepped into the cool, air-conditioned office, clicked my heels and gave my best ceremonial salute.

After an ominous silence he began hesitantly, 'Ah, yes,' his voice holding the tone of a vicar about to administer a blessing. There was another pause, then, 'It seems that your mother is seriously ill. I'm afraid death is imminent. Of course, we'll put you on the first available flight home.'

These words left me numb. I felt nothing. I can't

remember if I spoke at all and it was only after stepping back into the brilliant African sunlight that it fully registered in my mind just what had been said.

My mother ill! Death imminent – within the month! But she wrote regularly and never hinted at any illness in her letters, at least not her own. Since joining the army five years earlier my family numbers had depleted. First my sickly cousin died, followed shortly by my great grandmother. Then my aunt Jane and 'mad uncle Bob' died. The most recent had been my grandfather. My older brother Joe was now married and the only ones left in that big house were my grandmother, my parents and my little sister, Elizabeth.

I began to brighten up a little. Now, with so much room to spare and all the old family squabbles at an end, could this be a ploy to get me home? My family knew how I regretted enlisting. Had they pulled strings? But how? They had neither money, influence nor power. Confusion raced around my brain.

The adjutant was as good as his word. There was an RAF flight in at the airstrip and within an hour I was documented, packed and on my way home. The almost non-stop forty-eight hour flight dragged on seemingly to infinity until we touched down at an RAF base in Wiltshire in the south of England. From there it was train all the way to St Helens in the north.

On arriving home I was so fatigued the whole episode felt like a nightmare. But I was soon jolted back to reality when I walked into the house and my mother wasn't there. She really was ill in hospital. I remembered all the concern four years ago when she had Elizabeth so late on in life. Now I was told why. It was because she had a heart complaint.

After getting a bite to eat, having a wash and changing my clothes – still in a daze – I set off to visit her. She accepted my story about being home on leave and, so far as I know, never suspected that I'd been sent for.

Four weeks after my hurried return from Africa I woke up one night to a terrible noise. At first I put my head under the sheets to blot out the sound but the pounding persisted. Then I glanced at my watch on the bedside table and wondered who on earth was hammering on our door at four-thirty in the morning. With my heart pounding with apprehension I got up and went down the stairs bare footed. For all my army training and self defence skills I wasn't too eager to open the door at that hour yet knew there was no alternative. Whoever it was intended getting some response.

The policeman simply stood there. He said nothing. He didn't need to. His face told the whole story.

'It's my mother, isn't it?' I mumbled. 'Is she dead?'

'No, lad,' he replied sympathetically 'but you're to go to the hospital right away.'

For a moment I stood in silence, not wanting to accept what was happening. She had been getting better. This was the first good night's sleep I'd had because I thought her condition was improving.

I went to rouse my father and in silence we dressed ready to go. There was no transport available at that time in the morning so we made our way to the hospital on foot. We must have looked the odd pair; him in pit boots, flat cap and donkey-jacket, me in desert sandals and cotton trousers.

Throughout the three mile walk I prayed as never before in my life, 'Oh, God, please make her better.' I repeated this over and over again but my prayers were not answered.

When we arrived the night ward sister ushered us into a side room to tell us as gently as she could that we were too late. My mother had just died.

Until that moment, for me, death was a matter of fact; something which came to us all sooner or later. Even the deaths of my elderly relatives had made no impression on me. Now in the still darkness of a hospital room all that was changed. The muscles in my stomach began to contract and my inside churned. Fear of the unknown enveloped me, reducing me to a blind panic as the full impact of my mother's death hit me.

'Oh, Lord, God. Why?' I cried. 'Why? Why?' But in those awful moments there was no answer.

My father, never one to display his emotions, appeared quite unmoved yet I knew well the turmoil going on inside his heart.

There was nothing to do but escort him home; back to a house that was no stranger to death and once again its walls were filled with grief.

Throughout that day there were many harrowing obligations to attend to. Relatives needed to be told and funeral arrangements had to be made. With my mother in hospital, my little sister had been staying with our brother, Joe. Someone took her to school that morning but at lunchtime it fell to me to go and collect her and to tell her what had happened.

Waiting at the school gates, I went over and over in my mind, just how I could tell her. Would she understand? *Did I understand?*

She skipped towards me, laughing, her fair curls bobbing and her eyes shining. A great, choking lump formed in my throat as I clasped her hand and walked on a few yards while she chattered away, telling me of the morning's activities.

We were nearing home. In the old tradition our window curtains – and all the other curtains in the street – were drawn. When we walked in, she would see the house in semi-darkness and wonder why. I couldn't delay telling her any longer.

Struggling to hide my emotions, I said, 'Your mummy went to heaven this morning.'

'Does that mean she's gone to Jesus?' she asked brightly.

'Yes, that's right.' I looked down at her innocent

upturned face which provoked my tears. Before they began to flow I glanced towards the cloudless sky and silently asked, 'What God can do this?'

In those moments the seeds of atheism were sown. I began to challenge the entire concept of Christianity and in God himself.

Attended by all our relatives, friends and many neighbours, the funeral took place a few days later at St Helens Cemetery.

Naively I thought the heartache would pass after the funeral but it didn't. My faith in God, together with all the security my Catholic upbringing had given me, was shattered. Without my faith there was no consolation.

Bouts of depression set in. Part of me simply refused to believe that, at forty-seven, my mother was dead. Through all kinds of weather I was spending long, lonely hours at the graveside. Hours during which, in a desperate attempt to communicate with her, thoughts of spiritualism and the occult ran amok in my mind.

There was even a time when, in my desperation to join her, I seriously considered suicide. The one deterrent was, if there was no God I wouldn't join my mother if I died because there couldn't be an after-life either.

The army had been more than generous, granting me three months compassionate leave, giving me ample time to help my father get his life reorganised.

Within five years, from a house teeming with people, the numbers were now reduced to two; my grandmother and my father. My brother and sister-in-law were going to bring Elizabeth up and I was returning to continue my ill-chosen career.

My regiment was due to return from Swaziland within weeks of my compassionate leave expiring so, instead of being sent back to Africa, I was posted up to Catterick in Yorkshire again to await their return.

9: Peace Keepers

In 1967, Colonel Gamal Abdel Nasser, head of the Egyptian army and President of the Federation of Arab states, was taking a great deal of interest in a certain piece of real estate.

After decades of ruling Aden from the corridors of Whitehall, although there was nothing official, the British were showing all the signs of preparing to leave with the intention of handing over control to local government. Colonel Nasser was eager to step in and end the 'tyranny of the British'.

However, before he could set himself up as 'saviour to the suffering multitudes', and relieve them of their poverty and deprivation, he needed to convince them of his God-given right to take control of the nation.

Before anyone was aware of the situation and able to stem the flow, his supporters had infiltrated the South Yemen in alarming numbers. Terrorist groups were set up and, to drive the 'oppressive Britons' from the land, violence was brought to the streets of Aden.

When our Commanding Officer announced that we were off to this hotbed of revolution, it was February and we were busy playing snow soldiers on the desolate Yorkshire moors. In no time we had exchanged our winter warfare suits for more appropriate apparel and were leaving England's fogbound shores en route for the sweltering heat of the Arabian peninsula.

It was 3 am when the plane reached its destination but the airport was a scene of frenzied activity with military guards armed to the teeth.

Customs formalities were dispensed with and we were quickly ushered aboard a vehicle which can only be described as resembling a caged porcupine. The bus was enclosed in a wire mesh from which protruded dozens of rifles and radio aerials.

We were housed right in the centre of our operations area at Canute Barracks in the downtown district of Twahi. This was during the Beatles era and due to the number of Liverpool lads stationed there the barracks was nicknamed 'The Yellow Submarine'.

From there, throughout the twenty-four hours of each day, patrols went out to scour the criss cross pattern of tenement-flanked streets and narrow alleys of makeshift shacks built atop empty oil drums.

The scars of my mother's death were still with me but now I was beginning to think maybe my anger against and dismissal of God had been unreasonable. I needed spiritual support and began to reassess the whole concept of Christianity. But then, one after another, I was to see friends cut down in the prime of life.

Our first major incident came late one evening. In the oppressive heat and tension there had been an unnatural quiet for the best part of an hour when suddenly there was a deafening explosion followed by the crack of gunfire. Without waiting for a radio message I grabbed my medical satchel and made a dash for the Land Rover.

For seemingly endless minutes we drove through a maze of reeking, squalid streets. Not a living soul was to be seen until eventually we came upon an injured soldier lying in a pool of his own blood.

Shielded by a ring of soldiers whose knuckles pressed hard and white against the trigger guard of their weapons, I carried out some basic first-aid. Then the rest of my team lifted him on to a stretcher and into the Land Rover bound for the hospital, some five minutes away.

In those few moments I wouldn't have been any Arab

who might accidentally stroll into view.

From then on, never knowing where or when another attack would be, the street patrols became a battle of nerves and wits. As the number of incidents increased I was treating every type of injury – grenade wounds, simple flesh wounds or, sometimes, bullet-riddled bodies.

On a number of these occasions I narrowly escaped injury myself. Perhaps this was what started me looking to God again, carrying him in my thoughts; murmuring a short prayer from time to time.

On June 6th, 1967, while I was sitting in the barracks courtyard, the BBC newsreader on the world service calmly announced that the combined forces of Egypt, Syria and Jordan were at war with the state of Israel.

'Blimey,' someone yelled across the yard 'Old Nasser's taken the Jews on.'

'Israel, where's that?' I asked.

'It's the Holy Land, Jerusalem.'

I knew of the *Holy Land*, Jerusalem, Galilee and Nazareth were all places associated with Jesus. But Israel?

My biblical geography lesson was brought to an abrupt end when someone shouted that we had been put on Red Alert – the code used by the security forces for imminent danger. If my knowledge of the Old Testament was vague it was about to be improved in a drastic lesson.

Aden may have been far from Israel's borders but within its boundaries – and particularly in our operational area – there lived a large Jewish population.

Perched on high in the mosque facing Canute Barracks, the mullah was bringing his evening prayer session to a close when crowds began to gather in the main shopping centre below. I knew no Arabic but from the inflection in his voice and the crowd's excited reaction I could sense he was inciting them to riot.

As the mob raged and chanted they gathered around the Jewish owned and staffed Marina Hotel.

Suspecting trouble, instructions were to get there and quick. But by the time the troops from across the road arrived, flames were already leaping into the sky. There was a complete absence of local fire-fighting equipment so while waiting for our own to arrive we could only stand back and wait.

The rioters soon made it apparent they weren't satisfeid with the destruction of mere stone and timber. They wanted blood be it Jewish or British and it took hundreds of CS anti-riot gas canisters plus the chatter of machine-guns to disperse them.

Until that day, the Jews had never been of any consequence to me except that as a child I was taught they were the people who killed Jesus. Now, while they surveyed the devasation to the once fine hotel, my heart went out to them.

That incident was the beginning of a campaign which included Jewish stores being burned and looted. Jewish nationals were verbally abused and threatened – sometimes killed in the streets.

And in those moments, witnessing their sadness and abject misery, I instinctively knew – there was *something very special* about these people.

The evening following the arson attack on the Marina Hotel I was in the small radio room we called the 'sweat box' talking to my friend Charlie. He also came from Lancashire and had been married just before leaving for Aden. Looking up at the wall-clock he got to his feet saying, 'I'm due out at seven. I'll see you later.'

'Right, Charlie,' I said and with our conversation at an end I tossed an empty Cola can into the dustbin and picked up a book.

It was ten minutes later when we heard the now familiar sound of an exploding grenade. By this time my medical equipment was kept on board the Land Rover. Someone quickly gave my driver the location and we were rolling out of the barracks gates on our way to the scene.

The back streets of Twahi were charged like a stick of dynamite about to explode. As on the previous occasion, there was not one Arab around. Even the local police-station, a short distance from the incident, bore no signs of life.

Charlie was lying on the ground, his lifeblood ebbing away through a mass of tiny holes pierced in his chest showing where he had taken the full blast of the grenade. The drill was standard routine. I gave what life-saving treatment I could before we evacuated him to the nearby Royal Air Force hospital.

There, amid the suffocating smell of antiseptic and ether, within minutes of being admitted and whilst I was holding his hand, Charlie died.

A minute shrapnel particle had penetrated his heart. There was nothing anyone could have done for him.

Heartbroken, and yearning for the long days of boredom I'd once complained so bitterly about, I left the hospital in tears 'Oh, God, why? Why Charlie?' I groaned. 'He's so young and newly married. Why, God?'

A short while later I lost an even closer friend. Hoisting the decapitated body from inside his vehicle, it was only when I saw his uniform that I realised who it was and it took all my strength and fortitude to keep from either fainting or vomiting.

When, nine months later, the regiment left Aden, we had suffered four killed in action and over forty injured, some seriously.

I was awarded the Commander in Chief's Middle East Land Forces Commendation. But then, *I'd been fortunate*. Any one of those others had earned the same commendation.

From Aden, after some home leave, we went on an eighteen months tour of duty to Malta and whilst based there we made peace keeping visits to Cyprus and Libya. The entire year and a half was like a holiday and was in fact a 'reward posting'.

When the tour was over in May 1970 we returned to

England for leave before being sent to Northern Ireland.

After spending so much time away from scenes of terrorism and heartbreak, my mind and heart were somewhat mollified. My active Catholicism was completely gone, yet, inside I longed for the Lord I'd grown up with, the one my mother so deeply believed in.

But in Ulster, Christians – who all believed in God but in different ways – would go to their respective churches, pray to him, then set about maiming, torturing, shooting and bombing each other. As on the day of my mother's death I would look towards heaven and ask 'What God could allow this?'

By now I was nearing the end of my nine years' service and demobilisation was a matter of weeks away. It seemed strange looking back to when I first enlisted in search of travel and adventure. Within a short time my main concern had been how to cope with the long years of boredom stretching ahead of me. Well, those dull years I'd anticipated were filled to capacity with fear, horror, grief, suffering and death. From now on it was a peaceful, uneventful future I would be seeking. Or was it?

For nine years I'd known a rigid, disciplined existence where I held authority. And the excitement, the apprehension in all those years, could I really face a peaceful, uneventful future? I certainly didn't want to stay on in the army neither did I wish to relinquish my highly ordered life. The solution seemed obvious. I applied to join the police force.

10: County Police

It had been nine years since I'd stepped on to the train, leaving my home in St Helens to join the army. Now I was back for my demobilisation leave and would soon be home for good.

As I walked out of the old station buildings on that depressingly damp October day in 1970, it seemed nothing much had changed.

There was a town centre ring-road with a one way traffic system, and perhaps the buildings looked more weather worn and displayed an extra blanket of grime. As I neared home, there was one building that stood out – the beautiful St Mary's Church, Lowe House. It seemed a hundred years since my altar days; mass, confession and holy communion. Those time were all behind me now. I knew better than to put my faith in God. He was a myth.

As I reached my own road, some changes began to make themselves apparent. In place of many neat terraced houses, stood piles of building rubble. Even the Church of England school had given way to the bulldozer. Old memories flooded back of long, happy hours spent playing games with childhood friends in the once cobbled street now covered by a layer of black tarmac.

A sad smile crossed my face to think no one had bothered to mark the spot where the old oak tree once stood at the edge of the pavement. It seemed only yesterday when I had clambered up its long, firm branches only to fall off and break my arm. My mum was furious. I'd recently recovered from one broken wrist and there she was, taking me off to hospital to have the other one set in plaster.

'Oh, Bobbie,' she shouted 'you make me weep at times, the daft things you do.'

I could have wept then at the fact she wouldn't be waiting to greet me when I walked into the house.

No sooner did I arrive home for my twenty-eight days demobilisation leave when I learned my application to join the police force had been successful. I was to report to Hutton Hall, the Lancashire Constabulary Headquarters, in Preston – ironically the same area as my first army posting.

My first priority was to buy a car for the purpose; a battered, grey Ford Corsair which, within days, I was driving into the forecourt of the building, standing in lush green fields on the outskirts of the town.

When I approached the desk, the duty sergeant – looking closer to retirement than active duty – proved to be as benign as his appearance suggested. 'Nip and get yourself a brew of tea, son,' he said. 'We're not quite ready for you yet.'

Off I went in search of the canteen and eventually came across a set of frosted glass doors which bore a sign saying OFFICERS' LOUNGE.

In the army, officers' quarters were out of bounds to the likes of me. But this was different. I was here to be made a *police officer*. With that in mind, I pushed open the doors and stepped into the elegantly appointed room, my feet sinking in the thick brown carpet pile.

I'd just stooped to put my shabby suitcase down on the floor when a red-haired, red-faced girl came dashing over. 'I'm sorry,' she exclaimed, 'but this is the senior officers' lounge. You'll have to leave!' With that she tactfully ushered me out of the door leaving behind a group of officers all choking into their coffee and me realising there was a long way to go before I could join them.

The next seven days were spent doing some preliminary

training, being sworn in as a constable, and issued with a uniform. Then I was sent for a three months intensive course to the Police Training Centre at Bruche in Warrington, about seven miles from my home.

There I was taught all the skills of policing from simple report writing to attending a murder scene; from coping with minor traffic offences to the art of self defence.

At first it was a struggle to keep up academically with the others but my tenacity paid off when, at the end of the course, I came one of the top three in the class.

I was assigned to my home town and took up residence in the Police Hostel there for four weeks after which I sought and was granted permission to live at home.

At that time the Central Police Office in St Helens was housed within the Victorian Town Hall complex alongside the Mayor's Parlour and borough Fire Brigade.

When I reported for my first day's duty in March, 1971, the section sergeant bore all the characteristics of military training. Over six feet tall, a pencil thin moustache, neatly pressed trousers and shining boots suggested ex-guards and I prepared to flinch under his gaze.

'Now, lad,' he said in a thick Lancashire accent, 'are you the new probationer?'

'Yes, sir,' I managed to answer, struggling unsuccessfully to keep an amazed smile from spreading across my face. From my experience of army and police sergeants I fully expected him to turn livid with rage at my cheek. Instead he returned the smile and said, 'Right then. Come this way and I'll find you a locker.'

A week later during my first night shift as a probationer I was in for another surprise. We were in panda car Charlie Bravo Four patrolling the town's green belt when we came to a jarring halt. In a flash my colleague, who was much younger than me but far more experienced, was out of the car, staring down at an inert body. Although no stranger to violent death, I was in a state of nerves at the prospect of facing my first murder case. That was until I caught a waft of stale beer coming from the man and realised he was not dead – only dead drunk. I remembered the procedure for such occasions – he must be either locked up for the night or put into a place of safety.

It was approaching break time. There was a game of snooker due and there was no way my colleague was going to miss it. This was my first lesson in *practical* police work. We made a thorough search of the 'body' to find a set of house keys, a wallet with some scraps of paper and a diary containing an address.

Bundling the man into the car, we sped off in the direction of his home on a modern council estate. Using his front door key we managed to get him inside, deposited him 'in a safe place' on a settee in the sitting-room then tip-toed from the house, heading for a well earned break and a game of snooker.

We were still congratulating ourselves on our quick thinking and benevolence when an urgent call came over the radio telling us to make our way, in all haste – *to the address we'd just left*. From an upstairs window a woman was screaming loud enough to wake the entire neighbourhood, 'He's downstairs – and he's drunk!'

The complainant, an elderly widow, had just moved into the house. The drunk was the *previous tenant*! We'd deposited him in a house that was no longer his!

Had there been Oscars for acting handed out that night my colleague would have earned one. We certainly didn't let on to the lady the part we'd played in her trauma.

There were many humorous incidents in the course of a week's work. One night I was sent out alone to search the local cemetery in search of a missing man. Ghosts or the supernatural had never played any part in my imagination, but I wasn't sorry to return to the familiar atmosphere of the station even though it was to report the man was nowhere to be found.

My relief was short lived when a grumpy sergeant ordered me to go back and make a detailed search. This time it wasn't from the cosy interior of the car behind powerful headlights but on foot with a torch amongst the gravestones, examining every irregular shape and stone angel. Still no sign of the missing man.

Again I returned to report but the sergeant was nowhere around and I didn't put myself out to find him. At last, when my stint of duty came to an end I was just leaving the station when I heard him calling me. My blood froze. He couldn't send me back for *another* search, could he, I wondered as I went to report on my latest failure. To this day I can't decide if I was angry or pleased to hear the 'missing person' had been found asleep in bed at home.

Another time I was involved in trying to restrain a man making one of his regular axe attacks on his home and family. How that reminded me of my childhood with mad uncle Bob.

Of course not all the incidents were funny. Towards the end of my first year's service a call came in late one night to investigate an activated burglar alarm at a chemist's shop.

On arriving at the premises it was nine o'clock, already pitch dark and access to the rear of the shop was down a long, narrow entry, putrid from the stench of alley-cats and half-filled dustbins. Noting that the back gate was in a dilapidated condition I was about to put my shoulder to it when there came a faint scraping sound from the other side. My heart beat a tattoo and in the moment's hesitation, before I could draw my truncheon, the gate swung open.

In the same instant the moon came out to reveal three leather-jacketed youths confronting me. Two of them carried sacks. The third held a long, steel screwdriver poised above his head in such a manner as to make it obvious he was prepared to plunge it into anyone who got in his way of escape.

Morning headlines flashed before my eyes 'CONSTABLE MURDERED WHILST FOILING DRUGS RAID'.

'Now, son,' I coaxed, 'don't do anything silly. Put it down.'

The lad glanced at his companions then at me before slowly lowering his hand and offering me the lethal weapon. In the time it took reinforcements to arrive we all talked quite amicably but how I don't know. My nerves were shattered and my heart thumped so I was sure they could hear it.

It had been a long time since I'd prayed but out of sheer terror, without even realising it, I prayed that night.

Afterwards I felt stupid. Why *pray* for help when there was no God? Doubts built up in my mind. Only God could have prevented the lad from using that screwdriver and only God could have put the words into my mouth which persuaded him not to. I was powerless to think such rhetoric let alone voice it. I was even more convinced of God's hand in the drama on learning later that the lads were heavily drugged and, in that state, were capable of anything.

Maybe God was there after all.

It was one night during my probationary period that a friend invited me to his twenty-first birthday party. I went along in the hope of meeting friends from the past but on arriving there, my gaze fell upon a girl sitting in a far corner, and for the rest of the evening I was oblivious to anyone else.

Maureen was a beautiful blonde with a creamy complexion and hair that cascaded aound her shoulders. Her demure, white blouse was teamed with a long green skirt which exactly matched and emphasised the green of her eyes that were more soft and gentle than ever I'd seen.

Until that night I would have scoffed at the very notion of 'love at first sight'. But that is exactly what it was. We spent the evening together and when I asked her out the following evening she took my breath away by saying 'Yes'.

That shock was nothing compared to the one I received the next night. She'd borrowed her father's car and we drove to an out of town pub. There we sat, telling each other our life stories. Maureen was nineteen, lived locally and was a post-office telephonist.

It was her age that bothered me. I was twenty-seven. Was it possible that such a beautiful girl – and one so young – could be attracted to me? No. Of course not, I thought. But one more hour of her company and my emotions refused to be controlled.

'Will you marry me?' I suddenly blurted out.

She turned to gaze at me for a moment with her beautiful eyes and said 'Yes'!

Right there and then we began to make plans for our future together. We would set a date for a year hence. This would give us ample opportunity to save some money and really get to know each other well.

The second consideration was, where would we marry? I didn't care, yet at the back of my mind, I had a romantic vision of Maureen being married in white in a little, picturesque, country church.

I put this suggestion to her and it was precisely what she wanted. It transpired that Maureen was a deeply committed Christian whose unquestioning faith put me to shame. The fact she belonged to the Church of England rather than the Catholic church meant nothing to me.

'Is she a Catholic?' my father asked when I broke the news of my forthcoming marriage.

'Is she a Catholic, Bobbie?' my hard-of-hearing grandmother repeated.

'No!' I snapped 'She's a Protestant!'

'Your mother would turn in her grave if she knew.'

I spun round on my grandmother but instead of saying anything, stormed from the house leaving my father sitting in his chair, shaking his head as though his son were guilty of some heinous crime.

There hadn't been one word of congratulation merely a harking back to the old days – days that were long gone from my life. All the old taboos associated with my Catholic upbringing came pouring out of my memory but they had no influence any more. Nothing, not family, church nor God himself would stop me from marrying Maureen.

By the time our wedding day arrived in 1972 Maureen's family had moved to Golborne, a small mining town just outside of St Helens where, to our great joy, the parish church stood in exactly the setting we'd dreamed of.

By then, family bitterness had given way to resignation to the fact that I'd long since relinquished my Roman Catholicism.

We honeymooned in Germany, Austria and Italy, returning home to live in a police-house in St Helens from where I spent a month working in the CID. Six months later we bought our own home in Ashton-in-Makerfield, a little mill town situated about half-way between St Helens and Golborne.

It was just at this time when I completed my two years' probation and, determined to get on in the service, I applied for the Traffic Department.

In there all I needed was to keep my record clean and book as many people as possible. Soon the bosses would be taking notice of this constable with a mind to get on and I would be made for life.

11: Dr Death

At first, rather than actually being a 'traffic cop', I was more concerned with the sun-glasses and powerful 750cc motor-cycle that made me look the part.

My first booking came one sunny afternoon. Close to some roadworks with a temporary set of traffic-lights I parked my motorcycle on a piece of waste-ground then lay in wait ready to pounce on my first victim.

It wasn't long before my strategy was rewarded when a Morris saloon car came along the road. On approaching the red light, the car did not even slow down but actually accelerated. I leapt on to my cycle to go charging after my prey only to be slightly disappointed on seeing it was a woman.

'Good afternoon, madam,' I began with the utmost courtesy, 'Do you realise you have just driven through a red light?'

'Why officer,' she said coolly, 'I always stop at *real* traffic lights.'

Her attitude made me thoroughly angry. From that moment on I began to get really tough: mere cautions were a thing of the past. Every type of offence, no matter how trivial, went in the book. Soon I couldn't walk into the station without hearing comments such as 'He's one of the whizz kids!'

My ruthless reputation was so well known, other police personnel sought my advice. Things were working out perfectly, just the way I'd planned. But then I began to experience a more grim side of traffic control: dealing with accidents, which seemed to happen at an ever increasing rate. Some traffic patrol officers spend years in the department without ever encountering a fatality. This was not to be my destiny. Much of my on duty time was spent in hospital casualty departments and mortuaries or knocking on doors, informing people their loved ones had just been killed.

As part of my probation I'd already experienced time in mortuaries with their air of sterility and smell of death that lingered in the nostrils for days afterwards. The necessity for this training is that whenever an officer attends a fatal road accident he is later required to identify the body as being the one at the scene of the accident.

My first post-mortem came after a suicide calmly walked under the wheels of a heavy-goods vehicle. There was little left to identify. But the memory of those pathetic human remains stretched out on the slab will stay with me forever.

There was a period when there was a death at every accident I attended. Within less than two years I had personally encountered twenty-eight fatal accidents. No sooner was the report on one completed when I was writing out another and my colleagues dubbed me 'Dr Death'.

Naturally all this macabre activity took its toll of me. I began to have bizarre nightmares where it was *me* on the pathologist's slab awaiting dissection. In others I was placed alive in a freezer with a multitude of cadavers.

Eventually this affected my work and my health started to deteriorate. There was near constant stomach trouble and backache. I was irritable with Maureen over the most trivial thing, and began worrying how we would pay gas, electric or telephone bills – something I'd never bothered about before.

Two years after our marriage, our first daughter, Sarah Jayne, had been born. Now Maureen was expecting another child and, what with caring for a three year old and being pregnant, she had every reason to be tetchy and unsympathetic towards my problems.

But when I was in these morose moods, she was so

understanding and patient. 'Bob,' she would beg, 'let Jesus sort it out.'

One day, feeling lower than ever, I snapped, 'If Jesus is so good, why is he allowing all this death and sickness?'

'But, Bob,' she cried, 'Jesus means *love and peace*. It isn't *his* fault.'

Within days of this conversation I was driving along on a beautiful sunny afternoon thinking perhaps things weren't so bad as they'd seemed recently, when the force operator directed me to yet another accident in an outlying district of the town.

At the scene an ambulance crew was fighting to save the life of a four year old. Under the watchful eye of his father who was mowing his front lawn the child had, for the first time, been allowed to cross the road to buy an ice-cream. A motor-cyclist had suddenly appeared from nowhere, hit the child and sent him flying through the air.

The parents were distraught but only the father was able to accompany the child to hospital. His mother was eight months pregnant and had collapsed.

Fighting to control my emotions. I mechanically fell into the routine accident procedure. The child died shortly after reaching hospital and I managed to complete a full report of the incident before leaving.

From the hospital I drove the big accident unit out into the peace and quiet of the countryside where I drew into a lay-by and slumped over the wheel to cry myself sick. I argued and ranted at God calling up every blasphemous expletive I'd ever heard in my life.

That same evening, still on duty, I was driving the unit through St Helens when a teenage boy leapt off the pavement, landing right in front of me. I slammed the brakes on and almost fell from the vehicle demanding to know what on earth he was playing at.

'I don't want to live,' he mumbled, words slurred with drink, 'I want to commit suicide.'

Placing the handcuffs on him all my earlier frustration and anger returned. I wanted to lash out and thump him. How could a caring God choose to end an innocent four year old's life yet allow this scum to live?

Over the following years, my thoughts often turned to God. Never sure if he was there and, if he was, I just couldn't accept his methods. 'Why did he do that?' or 'What was his reason for letting that happen?' I would ask myself after some particularly harrowing incident.

I was becoming increasingly introspective and growing complacent about my work. Sometimes I simply couldn't be bothered booking a miscreant unless the offence was really serious. There were occasions when a missing rear light or the fact someone had forgotten to switch their lights on would be ignored – although I knew full well a caution would be as much to the wrongdoer's advantage as to mine.

One Friday afternoon in November, 1980 I arrived back at the group traffic-office. A shout came through the office window – 'Bob, the chief wants you right now.'

There was nothing unusual about that. I'd half been expecting it anyway. Every twelve months there is a staff appraisal when members are given the opportunity to talk about their problems. Also the chief can air any grievances of his own. Our chief had only been with us a short time but already earned a reputation for letting well alone as long as everything was running smoothly.

'Come in, Bob, and take a seat,' he said. For a moment or two he shuffled papers around his desk before he remarked 'Had a lot of illness haven't you, Bob?'

'Yes, sir,' I replied.

'Seems to have affected your work.'

My heart began to sink. 'Yes, sir,' I said, and held my breath in anticipation of his next words most of which I missed. The only remark I remember was

'Well, Bob, under the circumstances, I think it would be better if we had you out of Traffic Department and back on general foot patrol duties. Of course,' he added cheerfully, 'when you're feeling better you can come back.'

The rest of the interview is now just a haze, leaving me shocked and numb. It was reminiscent of the day the adjutant told me my mother was dying. This time it seemed like hearing my own death sentence.

Out of traffic after almost ten years. It wasn't the done thing to leave such an élite group unless for retirement or promotion. What would I say to Maureen? What about the gossip?

There were always those ready to ask, with connotations, 'Heard about Bob Carroll, out of traffic?'

Maureen was a great support at this time and tried to encourage me with remarks like 'God knows what he's doing' or 'Leave it in the hands of God'.

Sometimes I envied her faith. At others I pitied her for being so deluded.

12: Second Chance

After the abrupt termination of my promising career in the prestigious Traffic Department I fully expected to be hidden away in some undesirable backwater. Therefore my new posting came as a pleasant surprise.

Newton-le-Willows is a semi-rural area, steeped in history, referred to in the Domesday Book and situated about five miles from St Helens. I already knew its geographical layout and most of the men who worked there.

The force had recently adapted a new command and control system. This called for advanced drivers for the *immediate response* vehicles, dubbed by the locals as the 'Flying Chess Boards'. Out of 'traffic' I may have been but today 'foot patrol' means 'on four wheels'. And with my advanced driver's credentials still intact, I soon found myself behind the steering wheel again.

This time I was determined to put my mind to my work. There would be no repetition of laxity on my part. Fate had given me a second chance which wouldn't be thrown away.

The first emergency call came one cold, wet, March night while I was looking forward to the hot ham and egg breakfast due to me in a few hours' time.

A man, roused from his sleep, had peered through his misted bedroom-window to see three tough-looking youths in jeans and gaudy T-shirts walking stealthily up his driveway. He lived in an isolated, detached house and was thankful *they* hadn't spotted *him*.

As fast as wet road conditions would permit I drove to the house and had just nosed the car into the cul-de-sac leading to the complainant's house when a silver-grey Cortina, its wheels screeching, sped past us.

Beyond the trees in the drive I could barely discern the figure of an irate pyjama-clad man shaking his fist. It didn't take the genius of Sherlock Holmes to realise we'd just witnessed a car theft. I swung the vehicle round to give chase, my co-driver calling on the radio for reinforcements and giving details of our destination as I kept my eyes on the tail lights way in front of us.

The car thief was familiar with every inch of the roads leading towards Liverpool. He also knew every trick in the book to evade us. But after twelve miles, rouding a bend, he skidded and came to a sudden and undignified stop on the wrong side of a hedge outside Knowsley Safari Park. No one was hurt and before the three youths could get out of the car there were about a dozen policemen swarming all round it.

It felt good to be so involved again. After believing my career was at an end, I was back behind the wheel, had recaptured the old verve for my job and was more settled within myself than I had been in years. My hopes for the future seemed bright. The move to Newton-le-Willows was evidently the finest thing that could have happened to me.

I was still adjusting to my new area when the superintendent asked to see me in his office one day. Community police – a novel yet one of the oldest forms of policing – was being introduced into the division. The mode of transport was to be a pedal cycle and would I be interested?

One of the first lessons a policeman learns is to have a suspicious mind and at that point my suspicions were aroused. Was this a polite way of demoting me? My immediate reaction was to say, 'No, thank you, sir. I'm happy doing what I'm doing.' Nevertheless within a few weeks I had changed my mind and accepted the posting. It seemed they were looking for the sort of policeman who could deal tactfully and compassionately with the general public. Men who could mix well within the community and gain their confidence. What had at first seemed like demotion was in fact quite the opposite and rather complimentary. Needless to say, my issued cycle was a black, archaic Raleigh, something of an embarrassment after driving the powerful and impressive looking 'chess board'.

My new beat took in the ancient villages of Billinge and Garswood standing within a mile of each other. Billinge occupies much higher ground than Garswood and on a good day the famous Blackpool Tower can be seen at a distance of forty miles. Looking in the other direction the hills of North Wales are clearly visible on the horizon.

The work was made up mostly of stopping to chat here and there, getting to know local problems, the tearaway children and teenagers and the local villains.

It certainly wasn't the sort of work I'd ever envisaged doing but it was a beautiful district to work in and, once used to the job, everything seemed to augur well for the future.

I had a beautiful wife, my two lovely daughters, Sarah Jayne and Catherine, a nice home and a steady job in which I was gaining a reputation from the locals for being 'a decent cop'.

Yet despite all of this, there was something missing from my life.

I may never have discovered what it was had the young vicar from the local Anglican church not yielded to pressure from his parishioners. For a while someone had been stealing flower-vases from the graveyard and his 'brethren' insisted he lodge a complaint.

'There can't be much value in them, can there, vicar?' I asked, bemused at the fuss.

'Oh, yes. They're aluminium,' he said.

Now I understood his parishioners' concern. Enough vases melted down and the felon could make a tidy profit for himself.

With the aid of a driver colleague we began to carry out regular checks. This went on for weeks without success until one Saturday morning we spotted a man pushing a wheelbarrow towards the rear of the church, heading for the graveyard.

My pulse raced and from the tone of his voice over the radio, my colleague was feeling pretty excited too. He parked the police-car in a secluded spot and came over to join me. Under cover of two, massive, evergreen trees, we crept towards the suspect.

At one point my heart almost stopped when my radio sprang into life. It was set on the lowest volume yet seemed to boom out over the whole territory. I quickly switched it off but too late. The suspect had heard it.

On we trudged through a muddy flower-bed, expecting him to show us a clean pair of heels. Instead he stood glaring at us.

'Now,' my colleague said, 'what are *you* up to?'

We quickly established that he was indeed a local villain with a long criminal record. But it was a struggle to keep straight faces when he explained that, for his recent offence, he'd been sentenced to a period of community work. And here he was doing it—tidying up the churchyard.

All the same, he went to the top of our suspects list.

Travelling back towards Billinge afterwards, Dave, my colleague, suggested we put the information into the collator's office—a method of gathering criminal information.

Still in light-hearted mood from the episode, I joked, 'Perhaps we should add some biblical text to it—"Thy sins will catch you out" for instance.'

Without hesitation, Dave astounded me by quoting a number of Bible verses. He'd never given the impression of being religious in any way but the disclosure of this underlying side to his character certainly earned my respect.

Despite all my ever changing beliefs and disbeliefs, deep

down, I sincerely wanted to restore my faith in God. But some of the Roman Catholic doctrine instilled in me as a child was still there and I believed that if I ever turned to God again, I would have to go to confession. That was unthinkable. It would be audacious to expect forgiveness for all I'd done. Yet, as belief in God would also include the acceptance of hell, without forgiveness, I was already doomed to everlasting fire which wasn't a prospect to savour.

Some weeks later, while carrying out further unproductive graveyard investigations, I opened my heart to Dave ending with, 'I know old Satan has my locker and digging fork ready. I'm destined for hell all right.'

Dave listened patiently then said, 'For God so loved the world that he gave his only son that whoever believed in him shall not die but have everlasting life.' (John 3:16)

We talked some more but no matter what obstacle I presented to my achieving forgiveness and everlasting life, Dave countered it with more quotes until, in the end, he had me convinced – or almost.

The next day I was cycling along the busy main road when a request came over my pocket radio to go to a certain address as there had been something suspicious reported there. This could mean anything from attempted robbery to a sudden death. There are no blue flashing lights or sirens fitted to police pedal cycles but despite this drawback I arrived at the red-brick house at precisely the same instant as the area car.

At first there was only the quietness one associates with a secluded, little housing estate in the middle of nowhere. Then a neighbour appeared. 'He's in the garage, officers,' he said, with a note of reverence which could mean only one thing. Whoever 'he' was, was already dead.

Grim faced and without a word passing between us, we strode up the tarmac driveway towards the wooden garage where a crude note pinned to the door read: POLICE – USE

CAUTION – GAS SWITCHED ON IN KITCHEN.

After taking the necessary precautions we stepped into the garage with its sickly odour of North Sea Gas. It was a while before we spotted the body of a middle-aged man slumped between a blue mini car and the wall. The head was partially covered by a black, plastic, bin-liner while the end of an improvised gas-pipe hung loosely from his puce-tinged lips. Shabby, stained trousers and worn shoes told a tale of either poverty or apathy.

Obviously, as North Sea Gas is non-poisonous, the man had been suffocated by the plastic bag. In any case, in the early stages, all suicides are treated as suspicious deaths and it wasn't long before the back up services arrived on the scene; the police doctor, the crime officer, CID and finally, the undertaker to direct removal of the body for the statutory post mortem.

It was a sad affair, as all suicides are. In this instance the man's wife had died just twelve months ago to the day and his life was unbearable without her. The note he left read, 'It's not life I want to escape. It's my wife I want to join.'

Soon all the formalities were over with no one left except the neighbour, the stillness and myself. I bade farewell and set off to finish my patrol and to get away from that unhappy place as quickly as possible.

The nauseous gas was on my stomach and thoughts of death overwhelmed me. Pushing a police cycle along a country lane may not be the ideal venue for considering the prospects of everlasting damnation but it suited me.

In the eyes of the Catholic Church, suicide is a mortal sin and yet, on my mother's death, I'd seriously considered it. The official declaration of coroner's inquests echoed through my mind – 'While the balance of his mind was disturbed'. Well, my mind was very disturbed when my mother died. Could that be why I'd abandoned all my former faith in God? Was Dave right? Did I only need to believe to be forgiven?

The following Sunday, I was pedalling towards Garswood village to a background accompaniment of churchbells. The sky was cloudless and, taking delight in being alive, I surveyed the velvet green fields, gardens in full bloom and breathed in the fresh country fragrance that hung all around. Approaching the Parish Hall my attention was drawn to some hymn singing so I dismounted to walk past while I listened – at the same time mumbling to myself 'Bible nutters'.

Ten yards further on and I petrified. The most amazing thing happened. My cycle simply refused to move one inch no matter how hard I pushed. I finally abandoned my desperate struggles and I soon discovered there was one direction I could move in quite effortlessly – back towards the Hall.

Some unseen force was compelling me to turn round and go in there. In a state of perplexity I parked my cycle by the wall, walked up the steps and pushed open the hefty door. At my sudden appearance in full uniform a hush fell over the congregation. But once I'd spoken to some of them and asked a few questions, they realised I wasn't there in an official capacity and relaxed.

Only one still seemed disturbed at my presence; a man whose height and build would have looked more in place in a wrestling ring than at a religious gathering. He casually wandered over to me. I say *casually* because this seemed to be the impression he wanted to give yet I sensed an under-lying tension in him.

His manner was in stark contrast to his appearance and, for a moment, we gazed at each other in silence before he held out his hand and introduced himself. 'I'm Tom. Tom Sangster-Wilson and I'm a Jew.'

I unwittingly took a step back. I gaped at this gentle giant repeated what he'd said. *A Jew? In this place?* There must be some mistake. I'd misheard him.

Their service was just coming to an end when I arrived

and I was given a cup of coffee. While I drank it I was told this was the Calvary Christian Fellowship and that Tom Sangster-Wilson, the Jew, was *one of its founders*. Their services were very informal; more of a meeting where everyone sat around waiting for the spirit to move them towards prayer or hymn singing. Even to open confession if anyone felt so inclined.

At home, all through the evening meal, I enthused about this little 'church' in Garswood where they gave out cups of coffee and one of their members was a Jew who believed Jesus was the Messiah. 'And his older brother is a *Rabbi*' I kept saying.

Sure she would think me possessed by some strange spirit, from time to time I cast sideways glances at Maureen who simply sat there with an enigmatic smile on her face.

After we'd eaten, I drove into Ashton-in-Makerfield to St Oswald's Catholic Church and settling down in one of the back pews I prayed, 'Dear Jesus, if you exist, please, let me see and bring my family together in one church.'

13: Saved

One aspect of police procedure is to investigate incidents thoroughly in order to present the findings to a court in the hope of obtaining a prosecution. What if I applied those same principles to searching for the truth about God?

Over the next days I spent hours in the local library going through books relating to other persuasions; Judaism, Buddhism, Hinduism, Islam and so on. In my eagerness to find the truth not even witchcraft was overlooked. Then there were all the Christian nonconformist tenets; Methodism, Calvinism, Society of Friends, as well as sects such as Mormons, Jehovah's Witnesses, Christian Science and many others.

The Bible with all its Old Testament prophecies was pored over. In the book of Zechariah it said, 'So I took the thirty pieces of silver and threw them into the house of the Lord to the potter'.

Didn't Judas Iscariot take thirty pieces of silver for betraying Jesus then, when he realised what he'd done, threw the money down in the Temple?

'Father. Father. Why hast thou forsaken me?'

Weren't these the last words Jesus uttered on the cross?

'And he was crucified with thieves'

When the Romans executed Jesus, didn't they hang him between two thieves?

No less than forty prophecies, all made generations previously, had come true in the twenty-four hours leading up to the crucifixion. With these facts I had to be convinced of God's existence. How could anyone fail to be?

Now there was no doubt, I'd finally discovered the truth. But where was this *personal relationship* with God that people talked about?

I was shortly to find out.

As a boy, I was taught that Gospel Halls were places to be avoided at all costs and had my colleague, Dave, not invited me to his one Saturday night I would never have considered going into one.

The place was packed with people, all with one aim; to hear the word of the Lord Jesus Christ.

I felt no desire to pray but sat in silence during the service. After a while a warm sensation gradually began to engulf me. My surroundings went out of focus and I was being spiritually elevated. Nothing was visible or audible yet I was aware of a presence as though someone was standing in front of me, looking directly into my heart. Without questioning this phenomenon I began talking—not praying, merely talking, and *I knew it was to God*.

'Why do people suffer and die? Why do they make war against each other?' All the old doubts still lurking in the back of my mind came gushing out for I knew *he was listening*.

Then the answers were pouring forth. Most of the world's troubles were brought about by man himself. If everyone obeyed the commandments God had given to Moses, and if everyone loved each other, there would be no suffering, no war and no crime.

My heart was overflowing with warmth and emotion. If it didn't soon stop, I would burst. I prayed, 'Jesus. Father I have been a sinner. Please, come into my heart and my life. Forgive me. Forgive me. I so desperately need you.'

These words were repeated two, three, four times. Then the gaping holes in his hands and feet manifested before my eyes and I cried, 'Oh, God, I love you.'

Suddenly I was at peace as though a great, troublesome burden had fallen from me. Elation swept over me and I was saying, 'Thank you Lord.'

This commitment to God was such a personal experience I told no one until some days later when I broke the news to Maureen who gave that same enigmatic little smile.

Soon I could stay silent no longer. Inside I felt like a volcano on the verge of eruption and a voice was saying, 'Go on. Tell someone.'

That Sunday, I made a second visit to the Calvary Christian Fellowship in Garswood, the meeting place of those 'Bible nutters'. There, part way through their service, I quietly announced that I had come to know Jesus in a way I never had before. Spiritually, I was re-born.

Maureen and the children were so impressed at this change in me – always happy, no irritability, no moods – the next time I went to the Fellowship they came with me. Afterwards Maureen said, 'You know, Bob, the moment I set foot in that Parish Hall, it felt like coming home.' I silently thanked God for answering my prayer.

Needless to say, just as I had begun to enjoy my glorious new life as a child of God something dark blighted my life. I was working my beat at the time, going up 'praying hill' – my name for the stretch of road rising from Garswood to St Adrian's Anglican church at its picturesque summit in Billinge. It takes some twenty minutes to complete – ten at a fast cycle pace – and here I could talk freely with my Lord, praising him, sharing my love for mankind and sorting out problems.

Without prior warning there came a severe stiffening in my legs followed by dull, nagging pain in my lower back.

Next day I could barely place one foot in front of the other. The doctor was called in and suggested my having X-rays. The diagnosis was arthritis. In no time at all I was confined to hospital on traction with the consultant telling me there was no cure and I faced ending my life in a wheelchair. Depression crushed me.

Trapped in a bed with two heavy weights suspended from my legs and the threat of losing my job, my wonderful new world was suddenly tumbling around me.

A week later, while still on traction, my general health took an unexpected dive. Sickness, headache and dizziness swept over me. Injections managed to induce sleep until two o'clock the following morning when every symptom returned with a vengeance. I was too weak to call the nurse. The straps round my legs became shackles and I was travelling through some bizarre nightmare, alone, in agony and terrified.

It was then I heard the voice, 'My son, why not speak to Jesus? He suffered for your sake.'

I remembered once being advised 'If you ever need God in a hurry, call Jeremiah 33:3. It's like an emergency telephone number.' It reads 'Call me and I will answer you'.

I prayed with all my heart and was almost exhausted when he answered. It began with a lukewarm sensation – the one I'd felt in the Gospel Hall – first in my head then working its way throughout my entire body. The pain, nausea and vertigo ebbed away, leaving me to fall into deep slumber.

In the morning I ate a hearty breakfast – my first in days – and when the consultant did his rounds later, he ordered the traction to be removed. Four days later, I was declared fit to go home with the promise of resuming work within a few weeks!

One hot day during my convalescence, when all I wanted was to sit in the shade and drink cups of tea, Tom called at my home to deliver a message. 'Bob,' he said, 'the Lord has given me the wisdom to tell you, you are going to work among the Jews!'

I almost choked into my cup but tried not to show my surprise. Apart from Tom, the only contact I had ever had with Jews was in Aden at the time of the Six Day War. But in the short time I'd known Tom, the Lord had presented him with some extremely accurate predictions.

All I could think of to say was, 'Well, if that's what the Lord wants.'

As he was leaving, he left a Jewish magazine for me. I read it that afternoon then put it down and forgot all about it.

As a re-born Christian, I hadn't yet learned what giving oneself to Christ involved. Several nights later I began to understand when the Lord began to reveal just what lay behind Tom's message.

It was miserably humid. I'd had trouble getting off to sleep then awoke again at one o'clock. For a while I tossed and turned, still sleep evaded me. Eventually I got out of bed and went downstairs. There, late though the hour was, I dialled Directory Enquiries for 'the telephone number of a Mr Don Hender who lives in Southport.'

Moments later I was writing his number on the telephone pad, then I returned to bed where I immediately went off to sleep.

'Who's Don Hender?' Maureen asked next morning when I came downstairs.

'Don Hender?' I pondered for a while then recalled seeing that name in the magazine Tom had left over a week earlier 'Oh, he works for the Messianic Testimony in the north of England. Works amongst the Jews. Why, love?'

Maureen stared at me then at the notepad. Only then did I remember my nocturnal deed.

Later that day I rang Don Hender in Southport, a beautiful seaside resort fifteen miles from where I live. After telling him of my previous night's experience and that *I didn't know why I was phoning him*, he made no comment but invited me to attend a meeting of his Prayer for Israel group in Southport, which I did.

My convalescence was almost at an end yet I still wasn't feeling well. Still, as I hadn't expected to make any sort of recovery, much less keep my job, I refrained from complaining. When the time came to resume work the Lord would help me find the strength.

Now I faced a dilemma. I'd discovered an organisation

called the Christian Police Association. Established for born-again Christians like me, it provided a fellowship where Christians can share problems encountered in the course of their police duties. Could my health stand up to involvement in both organisations – the Prayer for Israel group and the Christian Police Association?

I asked for Maureen's opinion and she advised me to ask the Lord.

In my prayers I heard that inner voice again, this time telling me to apply for membership to the CPA. That afternoon I posted the form to their headquarters.

Within two hours I received a phone call from their branch secretary, Mark Russell. 'Bob, how do you fancy a week with your wife and children at Butlins holiday camp at Filey in Yorkshire?' he asked me. 'It's a Christian Crusade and all expenses are paid.'

Because of my illness and lengthy recovery period, the family hadn't been on holiday that year and I felt quite guilty about it. My CPA application wouldn't even reach them until the following day yet here they were, contacting me with the offer of a longed for holiday. For a moment I was speechless then managed to croak 'Yes, I'd love it.'

Throughout the week, I would act as steward and sit on the platform while such great evangelists as Josh McDowell and Ian Barclay spoke to their audience. How I thanked the Lord.

Whilst at Filey, I bought a copy of Josh McDowell's book – *The Evidence That Demands A Verdict* – and asked him to sign it. He did, adding the Bible reference Romans 1:16. I quickly opened my Bible to look it up and found the words, First For The Jew.

PART III
BROTHERS IN CHRIST

14: Hear, O Israel

Throughout all this time, Tom and I had met frequently, our friendship developing into a deep affinity.

When Tom first revealed that the Lord had told him He wanted me to work among the Jews, I never imagined just what that entailed; much less all that would occur in my life over the next few years.

From being the community policeman of two small, peaceful, northern England villages, the Lord was to direct me to the very heart of the Jewish people. I would go into their homes, to their synagogues and to their land where I would both laugh and cry with them.

A week after my return from Filey, feeling invigorated and ready for work, I went to an evangelistic meeting in a private house close to my home. There I met the world renowned Arie Ben Israel who was to give a talk about his life.

He was born in a Siberian labour camp of parents whose one crime was to apply for emigation from Russia to Israel. Eventually his family did reach the land of their ancestors where, in time, their son came to accept Jesus as his personal Messiah. Now living in West Germany his life's mission is to conduct a ministry of reconciliation between Jews and Germans.

Although his talk impressed me greatly I didn't expect the consequence when it came some days later.

First of all there formulated in my mind an illogical urge to learn a foreign language – Russian.

Next I began to receive mental images of people, a host of them. Dozens, hundreds, thousands of men, women and children all flocking towards a great ethereal gateway in some sort of exodus. Some were smiling, others weeping but no matter how forlorn, each face displayed a ray of hope. By night I dreamed of them. By day it was just a momentary flash, then it was gone.

It was all most extraordinary yet I knew it held some significance for didn't the prophet Amos say 'Surely, the Lord does nothing without revealing his plan to his servants'.

I made tentative enquiries regarding tuition in the Russian language but the fees were so expensive as to be prohibitive so, reluctantly, I abandoned that ambition.

A month after the Arie Ben Israel talk, while in Southport at a meeting of the Prayer for Israel group, I heard mention of a book called *Exodus II* by Steve Lightle. For some inexplicable reason, I needed to possess that book and ordered it the following day from the stocklist. They told me it was difficult to obtain but I was willing to wait.

At the next meeting of the Calvary Christian Fellowship, someone walked up to me saying, quite simply, 'I want you to have this' and handed me a copy of the very book I so desperately wanted.

Without knowing why, my heart pounded with anticipation as I raced home and sped up the stairs. Sitting on the edge of the bed I opened the book and my arms began to shake, then my body began to tremble all over. I broke into a cold sweat and thrust the book from me but as it lay by my side, words appeared to leap out from the pages; I am going to bring them out of Russia.

Russia? Them? Could this be the message I'd been waiting for? Did this explain my visions of an exodus and my longing to learn the Russian language?

'Oh, Lord,' I prayed, 'if this is what you want of me, I'm willing to learn. But, Lord, you know I can't afford it.'

Within days someone told me of a school in Chorley, about ten miles away, where the languages teacher taught Russion. I rang the school and discovered the teacher not only lived less than half a mile from my home but was a born-again Christian who was willing to teach me 'for the love of God'.

Learning the language was far more difficult than I'd anticipated and the pronunciation nigh impossible. Then as I was going up my 'praying hill' one morning, I almost fell from my cycle when, in fluent Russian, I began to quote phrases which had evaded me for weeks.

When I told Tom of my recent experiences he smiled and quoted, Jeremiah 31:8 'See, I will bring them from the land of the north and gather them from the ends of the earth'.

Within a week of that conversation, I was put in a situation which had me convinced *my own* time on earth was drawing to a close.

It occurred around 3 o'clock in the afternoon while I was patrolling Garswood village. As usual, I had been stopping to chat to shopkeepers, councillors, friends and neighbours. Invariably, during these conversations, my new-found faith in Christ would arise. In fact, some of the people were beginning to call me 'Pastor Bob'. This is probably why someone felt able to confide in me that a couple of my friends were dabbling in the occult and witchcraft. As hitherto good, down-to-earth people they were surely unaware of the evil they were tampering with and I felt obliged to pay them a call.

It was a short visit during which we shared a pot of tea and they proffered some local gossip for me to pass on to the police collator. I talked about my joy in being a re-born Christian and the only time we broached the topic lurking in the back of my mind was when they referred to a self-confessed *white witch* living in the next village.

Twenty minutes later I bade them farewell and went on my way. But within an hour of leaving their home I became aware of an intense itching on my arm and removed my jacket to see three small blisters. Almost at once, my left calf began to itch and there was an enormous blister which continued to increase in size even as I gazed at it.

As soon as my shift was over I went to the doctor's surgery. By now, the festering nodules were profuse, the first of which had become the size of a golf ball. The doctor was amazed and diagnosing an allergy, sent me home with some antihistamine medicine which proved quite ineffectual. By midnight, my entire body was covered with the suppurate growths. I felt so ill, the emergency 'on call' doctor was brought in who, on seeing my condition, wasted no time and once more I was being whisked off to hospital.

Within an hour of being admitted, pneumonia had developed. My temperature soared; breathing was laboured; my vision impaired and, when my wife stood by the bedside, I barely recognised her. Two other people were permitted to see me: Alan Abbott, a police colleague and Russ Fairhurst, one of the church Elders. Together they prayed at my bedside but my one awareness was of life quickly slipping away from me.

If the onset and nature of the complaint had baffled the entire medical team it was nothing compared with their astonishment when my fever suddenly left me and the blisters receded to leave not even a scar. Within five days I was recovered enough to return home.

I drew my own conclusions on both counts. The malady obviously came from the home of my friends where, what they believed to be an innocuous pastime, had opened the flood-gates of evil. Maybe if I'd made no reference to my faith in Jesus Christ I would have been spared the suffering. But Satan is known for his malevolence, not compassion. My quick recovery could only be attributed to my Christian well-wishers. I am convinced it was nothing other than the power of their fervent prayer which kept me from death that weekend.

After that strange illness, my thoughts were centred even more upon Israel and the plight of exiled Jews. In Tom I found a good tutor who brought the Old Testament scriptures to life and instructed me in Jewish history. I learned that in the world today there are over fourteen million Jews. Since 1948 when Israel, a country the size of Wales, was returned to the Jews they have been returning in their thousands. Even so, there are still half a million living in Britain; six million in the USA and over two million behind the Iron Curtain. The vast majority of Jews believe this world exodus, culminating in their people's return to Israel, is not the fulfilment of Biblical prophecy. They say, that will only happen when the Messiah comes. Most Christians counter this by believing all prophecy was fulfilled when Jesus died on the cross. Yet today also there are Jews who recognise the fact that *Jesus was their Messiah*. And there are Christians everywhere who find they are carrying an unaccountable burden for Israel and her people.

One morning when Tom came to see me, I could sense something was troubling him. I soon coaxed it from him. He'd received an anonymous telephone call, in which the speaker not only threatened him but promised 'to fix that Jewish policeman over in Garswood'. Of course, during my fifteen years in the force, such intimidation became a way of life. There was always someone going to 'fix' either myself or my family. I tried to reassure Tom that they were merely idle threats voiced in the heat of a moment's anger. But the expression on his face told of all the suffering his people had endured for centuries. Saddest of all was his stoical acceptance that there would never be an end to it.

A couple of days later, my philosophy was proved wrong and Tom's fears were justified. Anti-semitic stickers appeared on his car windscreen. On the car bonnet he found dolls impales by scores of pins. Dents and scratches appeared on my car. The tyres were punctured by nails and the radio aerial was snapped off. However, when police colleagues started making enquiries and began keeping our homes under close scrutiny the vandalism stopped and we were left in peace.

Yet again, my health was giving me trouble. My back ached constantly, sometimes going into spasm. There were visits to consultants followed by X-rays, tests and lengthy stays in hospital. People prayed over me, anointed me with oil and could neither understand why, this time, their prayers were going unanswered nor why I was content to accept my sufferings. The latter was also a mystery to me. My former illnesses were all accompanied by a sense of frustration and anxiety so why should I react in this way now?

Meanwhile, during bouts of good health, the church appointed me as Missionary Secretary. My responsibility was to collect information from various national and international Jewish and Gentile mission agencies regarding the work they were doing and the people who were working for them.

The response was extraordinary. Although there was virtually no information forthcoming from any of the *Gentile* missions, there was a profuse response from almost all of the Jewish missions. When I reported my findings, naively thinking any response at all was welcome, I was taken to task by a church elder for 'making things too Jewish'; yet it was none of my doing.

Emotion choked me and I could think of no rejoinder. On reflection I wondered if this was God's way of letting me sample just a little of what Jews suffered the world over.

Always there were bewildering questions hanging over me. Why should I, of all people, have been led to Tom Sangster-Wilson. Why the impulsion to learn Russian?

Why should I receive those visions of exodus? And now, why was it all *the Jewish Missions* who answered my enquiries?

Little did I know an even greater mystery was about to be presented to me.

It occurred one afternoon during a quiet prayer time at home. I became so acutely conscious of the Lord's presence in the room it seemed that by reaching out I would touch him. Then I heard myself singing with the voices of angels. After the singing, the words 'Friends of Israel! Christian Friends of Israel!' issued from my lips.

After a while, when it had ceased, I asked the Lord what it meant. Again, I heard those same words 'Friends of Israel'.

For weeks I kept the incident to myself, constantly going over in my mind analysing every detail of it to ensure there wasn't something I'd overlooked which would offer an explanation. I contacted the Gospel Friends of Israel in America to see if it was to them I was being guided. But their interpretation of the old prophecies were totally different from those I'd been led to believe in. That was not the road I was seeking.

Eventually I confided in Tom who suggested we go over to Southport to discuss it with Don Hender. Always alert in the knowledge that Satan sometimes masquerades as a guiding light, we all prayed and held several meetings to discuss it further. Finally we decided it was indeed the Lord who had put those words into my mind and on my lips. Now the time had come to share the experience with our brothers and sisters in Christ.

It was to be a small meeting in our home. Twelve people who were all concerned about Israel and the Jews would be invited and Maureen would do the catering.

That evening there was an air of excitement and apprehension as the time drew near when the first of our guests should be arriving. Then there was a slight set-back when

Maureen was preparing the buffet and discovered that, instead of the twelve chicken portions she had ordered, the butcher had sent only eleven.

'Never mind. I'll do without one,' she volunteered.

The meeting was a great success with everyone turning up. I spoke of my experience when the Lord came to me with those words 'Christian Friends of Israel'. To my delight, everyone shared my belief. God was asking me to establish an organisation bearing that name. We then prayed for guidance in its establishment and for plans to help Jews everywhere.

However the biggest surprise came at the end of the evening when, although *everyone* had received a chicken portion, there were some left over.

After that, we knew there must be another meeting. This we decided to hold in nearby Ashton-in-Makerfield, where the Bryn Christian Fellowship met. Although it had a seating capacity of 125 we expected only about forty people to attend – still a vast improvement on the last meeting. Again, with the help of some friends, Maureen undertook the catering.

For a brief instant, just before the meeting was due to start, my thoughts turned to that fateful Sunday over in Garswood. The day when, attracted by the singing of the 'Bible nutters' and finding myself physically unable to progress along the road with my bicycle, I first came through that door and walked into a new life. So much progress had been made along the road since then.

My two main concerns on that warm September evening were that this was my first venture into public speaking and that only a handful of people would arrive.

My worries were unfounded though for when the doors opened at 7.30 pm, people began to pour in. When every available seat was taken they stood in the aisles; around the perimeter of the room and in the doorway. Far outnumbering the figure laid down in the fire and safety regulations they continued to arrive until it seemed they would spill out into the road.

Trepidation about my first public speech was also unfounded. The Lord was speaking for me and when they heard of his plan to establish Christian Friends of Israel everyone was so enthusiastic, the movement was actually born at that meeting.

All my prayers of the past few days had been answered. And not only that. Once again, there was an added blessing. Forty people were catered for yet almost two hundred were fed.

Immediately after the launch of the CFI, my health deteriorated so much that I was spending as much time in consultants' rooms and hospital Out Patient Departments as at home. Consequently, my work suffered. Everyone was praying for me but as on the previous occasion their prayers went unanswered. Why? they kept asking.

Eventually it reached a crisis when I was told my complaint may become worse. Even if it didn't, it was incurable and I would have to live with it.

This would interfere very little with my ministry work but it was shattering news for a police officer who needed to be in first-class condition to fulfil his duties. A muscular disorder which, without prior warning, could render me temporarily immobile was a liability to someone who could be called upon at any moment of the day to grapple with or chase after some felon.

Inevitably, I was summoned to face a police medical and consoled myself with the prospect of a desk job. But even this was denied me.

The medical officer came straight to the point with the words 'Sorry, you'll have to go.'

The new policy was to have completely fit personnel in every department, thus increasing the numbers to be called out on 'active duty' whenever a crisis occurred.

For the past fifteen years police work had been a way of life, not merely a job. Feeling as dejected as on the day I was refused admittance to the army, I returned home to Maureen – ever my supporter.

That morning, while in her daily prayer and scripture reading, her text for the day was Matthew 21:28 *'Son, go and work in my vineyard'*. When she showed me that verse all the fears for the future that had welled up inside of me were driven away.

How could I have been so blind? How could we all have been so blind? The Lord hadn't wanted me to continue my police work. There were other obligations for me to carry out – the tending of his vineyard for instance.

From then on my time was fully consumed with ministry work. Don Hender, Tom and I were visiting many churches, spreading the news of CFI. If the Lord had blessed our 'blueprint' on that Friday evening in September, we prayed he would now bless us as we went about preparing the foundations on which to build a firm and lasting edifice; the Christian Friends of Israel.

The first opportunity to put our beliefs into practice came when a local church offered us the produce from their Harvest Festival to donate to a Jewish hospital.

We decided upon a Jewish hospital and home for the aged in Liverpool. After a hurried 'phone call to ensure they would accept these gifts from Christians, we were on our way with the car filled with groceries, fruit and vegetables.

The reception we received was rather cool accompanied by an air of suspicion until we explained we simply wanted to offer the hand of friendship, with no strings attached. When we told them of the CFI they were filled with curiosity. Why, after two thousand years, should Christians suddenly want to befriend and help Jews?

Our explanation must have been agreeable to them because we were welcomed into their midst just as any old and dear friends would have been.

Some time later, we were invited to show a video in Liverpool at a home for the physically handicapped. However, on the night, the video developed a fault and the film couldn't be shown. Our hosts then invited Tom to go on stage and give his testimony of how he had discovered Jesus Christ, which he did.

I was seated in the middle of the audience and when Tom finished his testimony, the audience appeared to rise as one person to make its way to where he was; all of them talking at once. Until that moment we had no idea it was a *Jewish* home and I was convinced Tom was about to be lynched. He told me afterwards he was sweating with terror until he realised the people were all asking questions about Christianity and were eager to know more about Tom's spiritual rebirth.

More and more we were moving among the Jewish people. We went to Synagogues in Manchester to show a film called *Gates of Brass*. Financed and made by a group of Christians it related the lives of Jewish Refusniks living in the Soviet Union.

The most memorable showing of that film was one evening when Don Hender and myself were the only Gentiles present. At the end of the film the entire assembly was reduced to tears. We naturally assumed it was sorrow for the plight of their people encaged in Russia. Then they surprised us by saying they were tears of joy that Christians were making such practical gestures of love and reconciliation to atone for all the past centuries of persecution.

Nevertheless, we did sometimes encounter an element of prejudice and opposition to our work – often within our local environment. Indeed, we were indicted as Christian Zionists.

At times it seemed there were two camps; on the one side were those Christians who were suddenly aware that God was at work in Israel and the repatriation of her people. Sadly, on the other, were those who believed God had rejected Israel, her people and anyone who stood alongside them.

I found myself becoming increasingly involved in Soviet Jewry and, with my growing knowledge of the Russian language, there gradually dawned a burning desire to visit the Soviet Union.

Many cities in Britain have a friendly relationship with their Russian counterpart and my closest city, Manchester, has such an association with Leningrad. It was there that I felt drawn.

Before mentioning any of this to Maureen, I thought it wiser to make some discreet enquiries and went to a travel agent for details of flights, fares and accommodation. Everything appeared suitable and I planned to tell Maureen that night. Yet, before I could pass on the information, events took an unexpected turn. It began when an inner voice kept insisting 'Not now. First go to Israel.'

I had always wanted to go to Israel and meant to some day. But I couldn't understand why, when the Lord seemed to be pointing me towards Russia, he should then try to steer me in another direction. Experience had taught me never to question the Lord so my plans were postponed. In my prayers I asked for some tangible proof that my interpretation was correct. Then I waited to see exactly what his next designs for me were.

It was a month later on a cold, Monday morning in January when they were revealed to me. Having been loaned a film to show to a group, as usual, I first ran it on my home video to check that it was in order. It was just after 9 am. The children had left for school and, with Joyce, an elderly relative whom we'd invited round, we settled down to watch. The film proved so emotive that at its end we were prompted to pray. Quite unexpectedly, during the prayer, Maureen leapt to her feet and said 'Let's go to Israel.' This in itself was strange, but when taking into account that Maureen has a horror of flight and has never considered such a move in her life, it added to the shock. Still, she was so enthusiastic she insisted we get into the car immediately and drive over to the Jewish Travel Agency in Salford, just outside Manchester.

On the journey into Salford, Maureen remarked how wonderful it would be to go to Israel at Easter time. Of course, at such short notice, there was little hope of securing seats for that popular period. We would require four seats for Maureen, Sarah Jayne, Catherine and myself. To our delight we learned at the travel agents that there were five seats on an El Al flight for Easter week in eight weeks' time. Joyce hurriedly stepped forward to say she would take the fifth seat.

Only afterwards when the children arrived home from school and gaped wide eyed as we told them did we realise the impetuosity of our actions that morning. It was as though we hadn't taken any part in it at all and had simply been manipulated.

15: The Way Ahead

The afternoon of our departure from Manchester airport was overshadowed by heavy, grey clouds; huge spots of rain; a delay of several hours because of bad weather over Europe and, due to a terrorist threat against El Al, the presence of gun-toting policemen everywhere. Definitely not an atmosphere conducive to embarking upon the holiday of a lifetime; two weeks in the ancient Holy Land.

At 4.30 pm when we finally boarded the El Al 707, we discovered conditions were terribly cramped. Further complications arose when we were airborne and Joyce, thinking the stewards were the pilots, became very distressed, demanding to know who was at the flight controls.

Eventually we touched down safely at the Ben Gurion airport in Tel Aviv just after midnight.

Three weary adults, two sleepy children plus a mountain of luggage were bundled into a taxi and conveyed to the hotel in Sal Ed Din Street where we arrived at 1.30 in the morning.

It wasn't before the taxi driver had piled our luggage up on the pavement and I'd paid our fare that we realised the hotel was locked up for the night.

We were two thousand miles from home; stranded in a dark, silent street somewhere in the notorious Arab quarter of Jerusalem with not a soul in sight. How we prayed. Sheer panic overwhelmed us, not least of all me with my physical disability and two women and two small girls to protect. Soon, Joyce and Maureen were hammering with their fists on the glass doors and the minutes it took for the half-dressed Arab porter to open them seemed like an eternity.

He denied all knowledge of our booking until I produced proof of our reservation. Even then, it took stern looks from Maureen and Joyce to have more effect than the slip of paper I was displaying. Shrinking back a little, he quickly grabbed a bunch of keys from the rack, handed them over and pointed the way upstairs. There was no offer to help with the luggage but that was a minor obstacle. At least we were inside the hotel.

By 3 o'clock, after undressing, washing and doing some necessary unpacking, we were able to get into our beds for what was left of the night. One hour later, at four o'clock, high up on Temple Mount at the sacred Dome of the Rock just across from our hotel, the Islamic priest switched on an amplified tape recording, calling his flock to prayer. Welcome to Jerusalem, I thought.

Our first few days in Israel were taken up with visits to all the places of interest. We climbed the Mount of Olives. We went to the official site of Jesus' burial place and also to the Garden Tomb, the disputed burial site.

We travelled into Nazareth where PLO slogans abounded everywhere and a brusque priest dismissed us from his church with a wave of his hand saying, 'You'll have to come back another time.'

The tranquil Garden of Gethsemane, situated in the heart of the bustling city and where the trees are reputed to date back two thousand years, was one of the few places where man hadn't succeeded in utterly crushing all sense of the divine presence.

Obviously there was money to be made out of tourists yet the ethics of devout Jews and Islamic followers eager to prosper from something they not only totally disapproved of but *disbelieved in* was a great mystery to me. As a Christian, I had never considered the Holy Land as being a 'tourist attraction' any more than I would expect a Muslim to think of Mecca as a *holiday resort*.

After such a depressing start we really looked forward to spending our fourth day with a friend, Rachel Towers. During her Middle East tour of duty, Rachel was nursing at the famous Haddasser Hospital. On her day off she was taking us to Bethlehem which lies just a few miles south of Jerusalem.

Visiting the birthplace of Jesus the Messiah is surely the ultimate pilgrimage for all Christians. Yet, when I stepped from our taxi it bore no resemblance to the mental image I'd carried through life.

Bethlehem, meaning 'House of Bread', stands in a rich, fertile valley surrounded by olive groves. March saw it sun drenched, blisteringly hot and arid with its roads lying under a blanket of eye-stinging, choking dust.

Lines of predatorial Arab street vendors waited to pounce with their variety of wares; anything from a small, carved, wooden camel to a sheepskin.

Ahead of these lay the entrance to Manger Square and the Basilica of Nativity; said site of the virgin birth. Close by on duty outside the tiny police station there were police armed with sub-machine-guns while on the far side of the Square stood an Islamic Mosque.

The Christmas card scenes of snow-covered houses and inns, of wise men and shepherds trudging through snow-covered terrain and the animals in the stable huddling together for protection from the freezing night was dispelled immediately and forever.

On reflection, perhaps this is a good thing. For anyone who harbours doubts that *Jesus Christ was a Jew*, then his birthplace in Bethlehem will annihilate such scepticism once and for all.

If its exterior was unexpected then the interior of the 'stable' with a great edifice erected on top of it, was downright depressing.

There was an ominous graveyard silence and yet, once

accustomed to the surroundings, one became aware of muffled voices and the squeaking and shuffling of tramping shoes on the stone floor.

There was no sense of spiritual awe and, despite the intense heat outside, an overpowering smell of incense endeavoured unsuccessfully to mask a dank odour of decay. In those moments, I felt as remote from Jesus, Mary and Joseph as at any time in my life.

After a few minutes we eagerly returned to the outside world all expressing feelings of sadness and regret.

Rather than preserve the scene and sanctity of the holy nativity, it seemed twentieth-century man was more intent on destroying it.

We returned to Rachel's home in the French Hill suburb of Jerusalem where we spent the rest of the day. At night we boarded a bus for the city centre where we would get another which would take us to our hotel in Sal Ed Din Street.

While waiting at the city centre bus stop Maureen was suddenly prodded in the back and when she spun round it was to find herself looking down the barrel of a rifle. A gun-bearing Israeli soldier, after gazing into a shop window, had taken a step back only to have the rifle barrel make contact with Maureen's shoulder blades. Although she was obviously startled and blanched with fear, he offered no apology but merely glowered at her from under his eyebrows.

She was still unnerved when the bus arrived some minutes later and he followed us on board. It transpired however that this was simply to eject an unwanted passenger who had set up a stall on the rear seat and was selling bread from there.

In retrospect, I suppose that incident provided a light-hearted end to a day which saw us all retire to our beds with a deep sense of dissatisfaction.

Two days later a petrol bomb was thrown on board that

same bus we had travelled on so things could have been much worse.

On the Friday we were moving on to spend some days in Netanya, a popular, nearby seaside resort, and as it was the evening of Shabbat, when all Jewish labour comes to a halt, we hired an Arab taxi to take us there.

Stepping out from the hotel on to Sal Ed Din Street to await the taxi I glanced up towards the old city walls and there I saw a vision which will live with me forever and a day. High over the battlements, shedding tears and with outstretched arms, was the Lord Messiah of Israel. And, just as one would hold a childs toy fort, cupped in his hands was a miniature of the city. A portion of scripture from Matthew 23; verse 37 sprang instantly to mind 'Oh, Jerusalem, Jerusalem, the one who kills the prophets and stones those sent to her. How often I wanted to gather your children together as a hen gathers her chicks under her wing but you were not willing.'

In that moment I too cried. Then the image faded and was gone. Our taxi arrived and we were soon on our way to Netanya.

On arrival we were in for a very different experience from Jerusalem. As we walked along or sat on the beach, on street benches or in the cafes and hotel, innumerable people came over to talk to us. When they'd established who we were and why we were in Israel, they opened their hearts to us inviting us to their homes and their synagogues. Again their main questions were 'Why are Christians wanting to help *us*?'

One lady, a retired schoolteacher who for most of her life had worked in Yorkshire, England, was reduced to tears on our meeting. 'I don't know if you will understand,' she said, 'but there was something in my heart which told me I *must* return home to Israel.'

We understood only too well. '*For God's gifts and his call are irrevocable.*' Rom. 11:29

Whilst staying at Netanya we visited Jericho which was

another sad experience. A petrol bomb on another bus had resulted in all the places of interest being put off limits for the day and the city was swarming with armed soldiers.

But if Bethlehem and Jericho were prime examples of anticlimax, Tiberias on the shores of Lake Galilee caught at my very heart strings. It was the culmination of everything one expects to see, hear and feel in that sacred land.

In place of dust-covered highways leading to the desert wilderness of the south, this part of Israel is situated in lush, green countryside. And where its surrounding hills sloped steeply to the water's edge, Tiberias compared favourably with our own English Lake District.

In the year 70 BC, Josephus Flavius, governor of Galilee, described it in a way which is still appropriate today when he said 'It is wonderful in its attribute and beauty. The soil of this land is very fertile and thus no plant on earth is missing here.'

During our stay we met and ate with local Jews and visited the ruins of the Herodian and Roman period. But the supreme joy was to bathe our feet in the calm, cool waters of the lake.

The lake, or Sea of Galilee as it is known locally, is harp shaped; forty-nine metres in depth; twenty-one kilometres long and thirteen kilometres at its widest point. In all a measurement of one hundred and sixty-five square kilometres.

From time immemorial the 'sea' has been noted for its abundance and variety of edible fish. It is phenomenal in that, without warning, such fierce storms blow up that many fishing boats have been taken to the bottom in a matter of minutes. Then with equal suddenness, the calm returns.

Man has made no impact there and the Lord's presence was overwhelming.

Sitting amid the ruins of an old synagogue, I read Matthew's account of Jesus walking through Galilee, first calling his disciples and then preaching in the synagogue.

By the shores of the lake Jesus was there, not only in the flesh two thousand years earlier, but on that March day in 1986. I could hear him talking to Andrew. I saw the nets cast upon the waters. I saw him walk upon the water.

My one sadness, over which I wept, was that so many of his chosen people are blind to the fact that their Messiah, for whom they have waited so long, is among them always.

First To The Jew (Rom. 1:16). Now I knew why the Lord had directed me towards Israel. This was the land where his son, Jesus, was born, lived and was crucified; where he was resurrected and from where he ascended into heaven.

Without that journey, could I have ever fully experienced empathy with the Jews and their desire to return to their own land. Even they fail to understand this strange magnetism which is pulling, drawing them home.

Since returning from the biblical land I have developed a sense of urgency in myself and encountered it in others. I have been given the strength to pursue strenuous Bible study and have twice attended Bible College seminars; all to obtain a teaching certificate. I am continuing to improve my knowledge of the Russian language. I am constantly meeting people who have the same visions of exodus as myself. From the most unlikely sources, fund raising for Soviet Jewry has greatly increased.

'He will raise a banner for the nations and gather the exiles of Israel. He will assemble the scattered people of Judea from the four corners of the earth.' Isaiah 11:12

Throughout Britain, all manner of practical preparations are speedily being made for housing, clothing and feeding Jews that will surely come upon us in transit to their reclaimed homeland—Israel.

Now, Tom and I; the once Torah-obedient Jew and the Roman Catholic acolyte; the former custodian of the law

and the reformed delinquent; the Jew and the Gentile –
brothers in Christ, are awaiting the day when the Lord will
reveal his great plan for bringing his children from the land
of the north.

And while carrying our burden for Israel we pray for that
other day, when all the peoples of the earth will have the
blinds lifted from their eyes to become one in Christ, the
true Messiah. The final reconciliation of the Jew and the
Gentile.

> My children, look to Me for I have chosen you
> to pray and comfort My ancient people.
> Look to Me, oh My children, for I am going to
> do a work in your day which will shake this nation
> to its foundations. It will be such a shaking
> that you will not believe it although you will see it.